To Matt,
You're the best & my favorite Durfee basketball player of All-Time! Thank you for your positive influence on my youth.
Dream Big Never Quit –

DREAM BIG, NEVER QUIT

THE MARC MEGNA STORY

MARC MEGNA

Marc Megna Publishing
1220 20th Street
Miami Beach, FL 33139

ISBN: 978-1-7334749-0-0 (print)
ISBN: 978-1-7334749-1-7(ebook)

Ordering Information:

Special discounts are available on quantity purchases by corporations, associations, and others. Please contact Marc Megna Publishing for more information.

DEDICATION

This book is dedicated to Pauline Megna, my mother, my hero, and a constant source of inspiration and support. It also is dedicated to two teammates, Walter Blue and Kenny Farrar, who left us too early. Their hearts and souls remain a permanent stamp on the world. I'm beyond grateful for the strong people in my life who taught me that the fire within the human soul is ignited by overachievers who attack life's hurdles with a positive spirit. That spirit is medicine for the world.

CONTENTS

Praise for

DREAM BIG, NEVER QUIT

"Within the first month of our becoming teammates at the University of Richmond, Marc Megna motivated me to push myself harder than I had ever pushed before. Today, 20 years later and living 1,500 miles apart, Marc is still a motivating factor in my life.

The first word that comes to mind when I think of Marc is 'motor.' If he ever took a play off at the University of Richmond, show me the tape. I know he didn't because I lived it. I spent most of my freshman season running from him during practice. Marc practiced every day as if he was in a game, and he approached every single play like it was going to be his last.

I think many people are scared of greatness. It can be daunting; I get it. It's easier to accept mediocrity. Many people I know chalk it up to genetics, thinking, 'Hey, it's not in me,' or 'I wasn't born with it.' Marc is a walking example that an unbeatable attitude and belief in one's self can take you a long way in this world."

—Todd McShay, ESPN football analyst and commentator

INTRODUCTION

The first day of the 1999 NFL Draft came to an end and I had not been selected. That was expected. I knew that I wouldn't get picked in the first two rounds. I went to bed that Saturday night knowing that my moment would happen the next day. That's when Rounds 3 through 7 were held.

I worked as a graduate assistant football coach at the University of Richmond and was living in a converted storage closet in the athletic facility. I woke up early that Sunday morning filled with nervous energy. I hit the weight room for my morning workout, ran over to the dining hall for a huge breakfast, and then hustled back to my room. I sat on a shabby mattress with the landline phone right next to me. Once the coverage of the draft started, my eyes were glued to the mini-TV waiting for my name to be announced and the call to come.

It felt like an eternity as I watched Rounds 3, 4, and 5. Commercial breaks were torture. Even broadcaster Chris Berman's voice started to drive me crazy as he profiled chosen players. I found myself yelling at him several times to hurry up and announce the next one.

When the New York Jets were on the clock in the sixth round, I got a funny feeling. I can't explain how I knew but before I could process my thoughts, the phone rang.

"Hello," said a deep and raspy voice on the other end of the line. "I'm trying to reach Marc Megna."

"This is Marc Megna."

"Do you know who this is, Marc?"

The voice was familiar. I had never spoken to him but I knew exactly who it was, and I couldn't believe it. "Coach Parcells?"

Bill Parcells was a living legend. He had won two Super Bowls with the New York Giants and was known for being one of the toughest coaches in the league.

"That's right, Marc. This is Coach Bill Parcells, the head coach of the New York Jets, and I think you're a good football player."

"Thank you, Coach."

"Do you think you can play linebacker for us?"

"Yes, sir!"

"Can you rush the passer for us?"

"Yes, sir!"

"Can you play special teams for us?"

"Absolutely, Coach!"

"Well, we're taking you with this next pick. Welcome to the New York Jets."

I looked over at the TV and saw my name flash across the bottom of the screen. It was unreal. My mind raced. I thought back to those cold mornings before dawn when I bundled up to run through the streets of Fall River, Massachusetts. I remembered my late-night sprints at my high school track. I remembered all the people telling me that I was too small, too slow, and too weak to compete. Most important, I remembered why I started playing football.

For years, I engaged in psychological warfare with myself because my father didn't want to be part of my life. When I was six, my father walked out on my mom. My mother sacrificed and worked day and night to raise my brother and me, but I still yearned for a relationship with my father. I knew he avoided spending time with me, so at 16, I decided that I would finally get his attention. He was going to watch me play football and he would see how good I was. That would make him proud and want to spend more time with me. That moment never happened; my father passed away, and his death changed my life forever. I developed a deep, burning feeling inside that made me push myself beyond what I ever thought was possible. It came with a steel-cut focus and hardness that I did not have while my father was alive.

After I hung up with Coach Parcells, I realized that the struggles throughout my life had built me up and taken me further than I ever could have gotten with physical talent alone.

The next person to call was my brother, Mike. "I'm happy for you," he said. "You've worked so hard. You deserve it, bro."

Hearing that from my brother meant the world to me. I always looked up to Mike, and at that moment, it felt like we were both drafted. He put my mother on the phone. Hers was the voice that I wanted to hear the most. At first, there was silence on the other end. Then I heard her crying. When she finally spoke, all she said was, "I told you!"

"I love you, Mom. I love you so much. Thank you for believing in me." We were both crying at that point. In her choked-up voice, she whispered, "You're my son. You can do anything."

Once again, my mother was right. My mother was always right. Pauline Megna made me the richest man in the world. When I was a small boy, it was my mother who told me that I would play in the NFL. Nobody ever believed that was possible except for her. Even I doubted what I could accomplish but my mother never wavered.

At one point in college, I lost all hope. I wanted to give up on football and move home. My mother picked up on that. She knew something was wrong and wrote me a long letter explaining why it was so important for me to stay strong and to keep going. It wasn't just about college football. It was about how I would respond to life's challenges after college. My mother always believed in me but she also made me believe in myself. What she doesn't know is that I still read that letter every single day. At the end of that letter are the five most powerful words I've ever read in my life: "Dream big and never quit."

Even though my playing days are over, those words are the foundation of my philosophy and my mission. Today, I'm 42 years old and the co-owner of three Anatomy Fitness locations in Miami. I'm a top strength and conditioning coach who has trained more than 300 professional athletes, but my purpose is inspiring and empowering others to be their best. I don't have all the answers, but the one thing that I know for sure is that if you believe in yourself, fight through the discomfort, and commit to putting in the necessary hard work, then you can make any dream happen.

I am living proof. This is my story.

> *"You got this lion, he's the king of the jungle. Huge mane out to here. He's laying down under a tree, in the middle of Africa, he's so big, he's so hot! He doesn't wanna move. Now, the little lion cubs they start messin' with him, bitin' his tail, bitin' his ears, he doesn't do anything. The lioness, she starts messing with him, coming over making trouble, still nothing. Now the other animals, they notice this, and they start to move in. The jackals, hyenas, they're barking at him, laughing at him. They nip his toes and eat the food that's in his domain. They do this and they get closer and closer and bolder and bolder, till one day…that lion gets up and tears the shit outta everybody, runs like the wind, eats everything in his path, 'cause every once in a while, the lion has to show the jackals who he is."*
>
> —Christopher Walken as Mike in *Poolhall Junkies*

CHAPTER 1

JUST A KID FROM FALL RIVER

"'There must be some kind of way out of here,' said the joker to the thief. 'There's too much confusion. I can't get no relief.'"

—Bob Dylan, "All Along the Watchtower"

Whenever people ask me where I'm from, I don't say Boston, I say Fall River. The responses I get often come with sideways glances and comments like, "That's a hell of a place."

A blue-collar mill town between Providence and Boston, most people know Fall River as the home of Battleship Cove or the gateway to Cape Cod. It's a rough city with a hardened group of working-class people. They are realists with a pessimistic outlook on life, but Fall River and its people are what molded me into the person I am today. I learned several things growing up there: I learned to take pride in what I do. I learned to always give my best effort. I also learned how to fight—fight for what's right, fight for what I believe in, and fight for the ones I love. When I returned to visit the city a few years ago, an old friend told me, "It's always nice to have Fall River in your back pocket." What he meant was that you can take the kid out of the city but you can never take the city out of the kid.

People born in Fall River tend to stay there, and my parents were no exception. They met in high school, married in their twenties, and settled down to start a family. My older brother, Mike, was born in 1973 and I was born three years later. For a while, we all lived in a tiny apartment, but when I was six, my father surprised us by buying a house on Rock Street in the middle of the Seven Hills. Mom was so happy that she cried. It wasn't much but it was a castle to us.

The house needed repairs and my dad thought he could do it all by himself. My father had a reputation for being a hard worker. A former Durfee High basketball player, he was fit and slender but sturdy with a thin mustache and a face you could trust. He held many jobs as a kid, and after serving in the military, he became a realtor. He drank coffee, smoked cigarettes, and rarely ever slept. He was always on the move. Whatever the task, he gave it everything he had.

As soon as my dad got home from work, he'd start working on the house, cementing the outside steps or restoring interior woodwork. Sometimes he'd be up all night. He worked like a madman. He would skip meals and wouldn't sleep. My brother and I tried to lend a hand because we both wanted to make him proud but I have no doubt we just got in the way. We took turns fetching supplies and bringing him water. When he told us to do something, I made sure to follow his directions to a T. After a few months, the work started to take its toll on him, and we could tell he was overwhelmed. He needed help but he wasn't the kind of guy who could easily ask for it.

Slowly, construction came to a halt, and he began to withdraw from family activities. Some nights he wouldn't come home. At night, I would sit with my back to the front door so I could hear if his car pulled up. After a while, he stopped coming home altogether. My mom would hide her tears and come up with excuses to cover for him but we could tell that she was devastated.

When my dad asked for a divorce, my mom took it hard. I saw a different side of her that day. She went through the house pulling every framed picture of our family from the wall and slamming them on the ground. Shattered glass flew everywhere. I hid in the corner and cried while I watched my mom curse out my father. It was traumatic, but I tried to calm her down. I kept telling her, "It's gonna be okay. Dad will be back."

My brother knew better. "Dad's not coming back, but it's okay," he said. "Lots of kids only have a mom."

Mike had a gift for telling it like it was and not pulling any punches. I was six and too young to understand but my brother was nine. He knew what was really going on. The divorce was hard on both of us but I believe it was harder on Mike because he was at the age where he really needed a strong male role model in his life.

Since the house was in my dad's name, my mom moved us in with my grandparents. I thought it was cool and I loved to spend time with them. Now we could see them regularly. Grandma Lambert was the sweetest lady in the world and never had a bad word to say about anyone. Grandpa Pe'pe was the enforcer. He had a short fuse and he could get scary quick, especially if he saw someone trying to do harm to his family. Whenever my brother and I got out of line, grandpa would whip off his belt, and we'd scramble for cover. Once he caught up to us, we'd try to throw each other in harm's way. I'm convinced Grandpa Pe'pe is where I got my mean streak. Still, there was a lot of love in our family and we all supported each other. My aunts, Theresa and Mary Ann, dropped everything and bent over backward to help my mom.

We eventually settled into a modest two-bedroom apartment in President Village in a neighborhood called the Highlands. My mom always wanted to live in the Highlands because the neighborhoods were safer for kids. She decorated the place to her liking and made it comfortable for my brother and me. Mike and I had to share a bedroom for the first few years, and he was the ruler of our room. Our Aunt Connie and Uncle Herb gave us an Atari but Mike was convinced it was his so I could only play it when he was out of the house. We had some epic fights. Every time we'd wrestle, it would usually end with him punching my arm until it went numb. Mom thought it was funny and would let it go on for a few minutes before she broke it up. In spite of the fighting, I loved my brother and always wanted to be by his side. I did everything he did, like a shadow.

My mom had to work several jobs to make ends meet. Sometimes, she would come home from work to check on my brother and me. She'd ask

My Grandpa Abe was a hero to us all. He had a heart of gold.

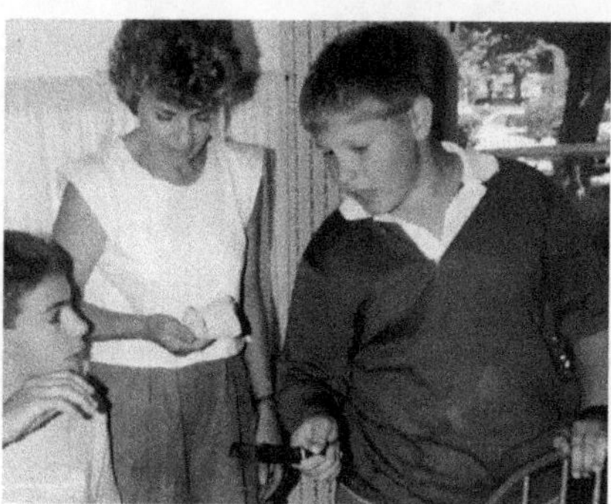

Not exactly little Marc. I was a dessert enthusiast and carb junkie.

My brother Mike looks like an angel, but he was always up to something.

about school and our day before she went right back out to clean houses for extra money.

Mom ran a tight ship. Mike and I always had a list of chores to do when she was at work. We knew how much she sacrificed so we were happy to help out around the house. Money may have been tight but Mom always made sure we were well fed. On the nights she worked, she would prepare food and leave it in the fridge with instructions for us on how to heat it up. On the rare night when she could sit down to eat with us, she would always wait until my brother and I were finished before she would take what's left. I couldn't understand why she ate so much salad. Later, I realized that she was making sure we had enough food. Her boys meant the world to her and that showed in every single thing she did. She would die for her kids.

Dad wasn't always there, but Mom made up for that with her heart and was always trying to organize family dinners. She even turned Super Bowl Sunday into an event every year. She would pick up a huge bag of crabs in the morning and then set up a whole spread on the folding table in front of the TV so we could eat during the game. You name it, Mom did it. It wasn't easy, but she never complained. She always smiled and was right there to motivate me when she saw that I needed encouragement. Growing up, I wasn't as popular or athletic as my brother, so I spent a lot of time at home. I attached myself to my mother, and she became my best friend.

Because of her love and support, we never knew what we didn't have. Before the start of school every year, my mom would make a tradition out of buying me a new pair of sneakers to wear to school. She would take me to Happy Feet, the city's best sneaker store where all the popular high school athletes went to get their shoes. The store walls were covered with huge Nike posters and pictures of New England sports legends like Andre Tippett and Larry Bird. I'd walk out of that store with a crisp pair of Nikes and a big smile on my face. When things got tough, Mom told me to look down at my shoes.

"They will make you smile and give you strength," she used to say.

Even today, I still look down at my shoes, and it makes me smile. Mom was good like that. She could make anyone feel comfortable. The older I got, the more I respected her courage and strength. Years later, I asked her how she did it all.

"It was easy. I loved my boys," she said with a smile.

"It must have been hard."

"No, I loved every minute of it."

I would not be where I am today without her.

After the divorce, my father was awarded weekend visitation so he would pick us up on Friday night and drop us off on Sunday evening. Even though we didn't live together, I knew he still cared about us.

My two favorite things: sports and dogs.
I asked for a dog; my mom gave me this one.

Some of those weekends were great. He treated us like kings and that's how we felt whenever we were around him. He was supposed to help us with our homework and other boring stuff but he always had a different plan in mind. Sometimes, he'd take us to the Brockton Fair. After we went on the rides over and over again, he'd buy us all of the junk food that Mom wouldn't let us eat. Burgers, pizza, fried dough, and ice cream—it was like we were in a fantasy world. He never did that kind of stuff when we lived under the same roof. He went from being hard on us to being easy, with less discipline. Other times, he'd take us to the video store so we could rent a bunch of movies. He'd then plunk us down in front of the TV while he worked. I didn't mind. I liked movies, and I was happy just to be around my dad.

He'd also take us to play baseball, and he was passionate about it. He knew everything about the Major League players and their stats. He spent hours helping to improve my swing and fix my stance. I wanted to learn it all, but he was obsessed with the details and had this intense focus when he coached us. We had to repeat things over and over again. Sometimes he knew that he was being too hard on us and had to pull back. I loved it when he showed up at my Little League games. He'd sit in the left field bleachers smoking his Kool filters. I hated baseball, but I went to those games because I knew he'd be there. That's what made me want to play. I couldn't wait to get in the batter's box during a game and do something special just so he could see me shine.

Fridays after school, I would sprint home to pack my bag for the weekend and then go outside with my brother to sit on our beat-up red bench to wait for Dad. One day, he didn't show up at all. I was concerned. He called later in the week to apologize, but it soon became a pattern. I'd make excuses, saying, "He probably got confused. Maybe he meant next weekend." My brother figured things out quickly. He blamed our mom for our dad's behavior and would make other plans. But I couldn't fathom the idea of our dad not wanting to spend time with us, so I would spend the entire weekend sitting on that old bench. I didn't want to miss a chance to spend time with him.

When he didn't show, my mom would get so upset that she'd break down in tears and leave a series of threatening messages on his answering machine.

He lived a mile away, so I would sometimes walk down the hill to his loft above the real estate office where he worked. I'd see his car in the driveway, and even hear him inside, but he would never answer when I knocked. More often than not, he didn't feel like being a father. He couldn't handle the responsibility of being a strong male figure anymore. It's like he took off his jersey and gave up all ties to the team, his family. I wish he had known how much it meant to my brother and me when he spent time with us.

My dad's life didn't turn out like he expected, and this left him feeling depressed. His personality changed. We had a connection when I was young but we grew apart. As I got older, he began to feel like a stranger. One time when I was wrestling with Mike in his apartment, he screamed at us. We heard him yell before but this was different. There was something violent about it.

Later that day, my brother showed me a razor blade he found under a speaker in the living room.

"You know Dad does drugs," he told me.

I refused to believe it, even though the evidence was right in front of me. Mike told me not to say anything to our dad, but I wanted to hear it from him, so I asked.

"Dad, what is this razor blade for?"

"Where did you find that?" he yelled.

"Under the speaker."

"It's for drugs, and they're bad for you. I let a friend stay here, and it belongs to him."

I was temporarily relieved, but we found another razor blade weeks later. We'd see remnants of pot around the house—tiny roaches and small bags of weed. We even found vials with powder in them. I didn't want to believe it. My father always told us that drugs were for losers. He said that we should never use drugs or spend time with people who did. He kept denying it when I asked but I knew that he was lying. My trust in him was broken. In spite of my father's flaws, I couldn't believe that the man I idolized did drugs, even if it did explain his recent behavior. He would flip out and lose patience, and he was no longer capable of showing us any kind of affection.

That experience shook the foundation of everything I believed. I learned that people lie and tell you things that aren't true. It sounds obvious but it wasn't. It was a hard lesson that I learned from my father.

WHAT I LEARNED

You are not defined by where you come from. Most people who grow up in Fall River never leave, but I knew I wanted something different at a young age. I learned how to capitalize on the positive aspects of my environment. My mom taught me about hard work, but the city taught me how to fight, and that helped to shape me as a person.

CHAPTER 2

SPORTS

"You must be prepared to work always without applause."

—Ernest Hemingway

In Fall River, sports weren't just a big deal. They were everything. The city looked forward to high school sports and invested in youth leagues. Every kid was expected to play.

I came from a family of athletes so my brother and I didn't have a choice. Our mom was always driving us to practice and games—usually an hour early because she was obsessed with punctuality. She was harder on me than any of my coaches, especially if she saw me dogging it. She used to tell me that something isn't worth doing if you don't try hard. It's because of my mother that I developed my reputation as a hard worker.

The one sport I desperately wanted to play was hockey. My older cousins, Brian, Chris, and Craig were studs on the high school hockey team, and I never missed an opportunity to watch them play. I begged my mother to sign me up for youth hockey at the local ice-skating rink. She agreed but only if I promised to stick with it for one year. She registered both my brother and me for the beginner's introduction course. Mike and I had a blast. Mike was outstanding but he preferred baseball and basketball. I stuck with hockey, and I loved it.

Saturday mornings unfolded like a comedy skit. My mother's alarm would go off at 4:30 a.m. She'd tell me to go downstairs and put on my equipment for practice while she went back to bed. I'd put on everything but my skates. I looked like the Michelin Man in all my gear as I'd trudge back into my mom's room to wake her up. She'd throw on this fake fur coat that she bought on the Home Shopping Network and we'd set off for the rink where I would skate for three or four hours. I practiced as much as I could and playing in the youth leagues helped me improve.

I enjoyed hockey and found my niche on defense, but sports didn't come easily to me. I was the fat kid in school and the furthest thing from an athlete that you can imagine. Mike was always a much better athlete. He was a natural at every sport he played. I looked up to him as my hero, but I always felt like my brother was embarrassed by my lack of athletic ability. I really was terrible. No matter the sport, I always had some kind of trouble. I liked soccer but we had to run a lot. I loved basketball but my bowling ball physique and two left feet made it difficult for me to compete. I wanted to play football but I was too heavy to play in Pop Warner, the youth football program.

Through it all, my mom did everything in her power to make me feel more comfortable. She knew that I was awkward and insecure. Whenever she'd take me for my annual physical with Dr. Gene LeMaire at Saint Anne's Hospital, he would tell my mom how I'd grow up to be a great athlete who would play in the NFL. It made me feel good at first, but I got frustrated because I knew they were just trying to boost my confidence.

For all the positive encouragement I received from my mom and people like Dr. LeMaire, I had twice as many people giving me reasons to doubt myself. My youth baseball coach actually told me, "Marc, I don't think sports are for you."

This guy thought he was Vince Lombardi and lived vicariously through a group of 12-year-olds. He didn't encourage my love for the game. It made me hate him and baseball. I was only a kid and couldn't figure out why he was so negative.

Practice was always the worst. I never had to worry much about the games because I rarely played, but practice used to give me tremendous anxiety.

I would tell my mom that I wasn't feeling well and needed to stay home. It never worked. I was glad when I didn't have to participate and put my shortcomings on display for all to see. What I couldn't know at the time was how the constant cheering and support I gave the other kids would wind up being a tremendous asset later in life.

Mom always told me, "It's good to move. You need to exercise."

Even my grandmother would take me on walks all over Fall River. Grandma had a motor. I couldn't believe how much energy she had and how fast she could walk. It must have been from all the food she ate. She was only 98 pounds but could easily devour three plates of pasta and large Italian subs without putting on a pound. I couldn't keep up with her in the streets, and she totally took the long route on purpose. She'd bribe me to tag along by promising to stop at the convenience store to buy a candy bar on our way back.

Mom and Grandma were right. I needed to exercise. I was slow, weak, and lazy. In my early teens, I was about 5'6" and 196 pounds. I was so fat and out of shape that I was petrified to go to the pool or the beach. When I went, I asked my mother to bring a T-shirt so the other kids wouldn't see my body.

Being overweight not only hurt my confidence and made it difficult for me to play sports but I also became a target for bullies. My family was loving and affectionate but I was regularly picked on by the other kids. It wasn't just teasing; they were physically abusive. I was getting beaten up and made to feel awful. Once it started, it only got worse. The bullying spawned more bullying because when kids see that another kid won't defend himself, they're going to pile on. I was constantly being called "fat slob" and "little bitch."

When I was 12 and we lived in President Village, I used to ride bikes with a group of kids from the neighborhood. One day while riding around town, we all stopped by the wooded area across the street from Highland Middle School. Three of the kids cornered me and teased me about my weight. At first, I thought they were joking but they weren't. They knocked me off my bike and literally beat me down. One of the kids whom I thought was my friend stood by and watched. Every time I tried to get up, I got kicked and punched even harder so I just stopped moving. When they finally had enough and left, I rode home with a black eye, crying. After that, I didn't

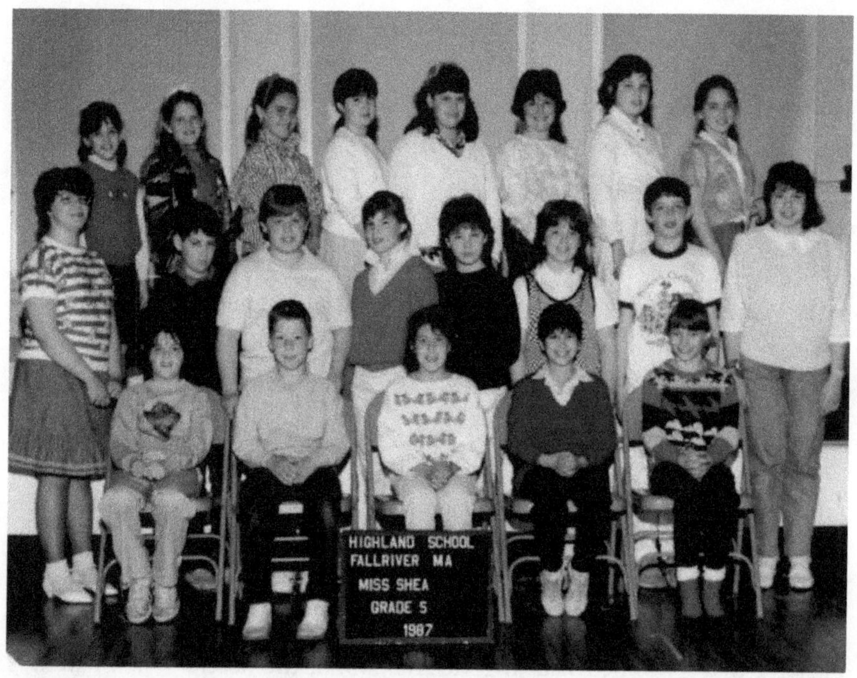

I'm just big-boned.

I would get excited putting on the Patriots uniform.

I started flexing at a young age.

want to ride my bike anymore. Some days, I didn't even want to leave the house.

A year later, we moved to the Rolling Green Apartments. We were told to stay away from the basketball courts, and one day I found out why. I went there with my friend, Ryan Olivera, and two older kids approached and asked us to play two-on-two. I was terrible at basketball, but it was a good workout and I had fun playing, so I said yes. Right when we started, I got walloped. I tried to call a foul, but they said, "We don't call fouls down here. Don't be a little bitch."

Okay, fine. Next time I got the ball, I went in for a layup and got hammered. I fell and smacked my head on the ground. When I got up, it was more of the same, "You're okay. Shake it off. Stop being a bitch."

We got the ball back and then I got clotheslined across the face. I had had enough and called the guy an asshole. That only made things worse.

"You're calling me an asshole?" he said, then kicked me in the stomach.

When I hit the ground, he started stomping me in the head right there in broad daylight. I left with a busted lip, a bloody nose, and cuts all over my face.

It felt like I could never escape. I was trying to play a friendly game and ended up getting bullied by another kid. I wanted to stand up for myself and do something about it so badly but taking that first step seemed impossible. Some days I would fake being sick so I wouldn't have to go to school. Something had to change.

My Grandpa Abe had given me a set of old weights, the type with sand in them. I had no idea what I was doing but I started lifting in my room in an attempt to get stronger. I was embarrassed and couldn't talk to my family about it, but my mother knew something was wrong, so she asked my grandpa to have a talk with me. That's when I finally told him what happened. I told him that I needed to get stronger so I could protect myself and go after those kids.

Abe White was an iconic figure in our neighborhood. Everyone in Fall River wanted to be around him because he was always smiling and upbeat. He was my father's stepfather, and he became one of the most influential people in my life. After my parents divorced, Abe helped out my mother in every way possible. He was always there to give us rides, and he would slip my brother and me a few bucks when he had it. He opened bank accounts for all of his grandchildren as a lesson in saving and discipline.

He'd tell us, "Add to this or spend it on something important, but regardless, remember how long it takes to build something important."

Even though he wasn't blood, he was family to me. He was the most caring, kind, gentle, and loving man I've ever been around because he always helped people and made them feel special. He didn't have a cynical bone in his body. I miss him so much. Today when I'm faced with a difficult situation, I'll ask myself, "What would Grandpa Abe do?" It's been 20 years since he passed away, but I still remember his phone number to this day.

When Abe was younger, he trained kids at the Boys & Girls Club. Most notably, he trained a local kid named Everett Sinderoff, who went on to become Mr. Universe. I remember looking up at a poster of Everett in the gym and telling my grandfather that I wanted to get big like that.

He said, "If I help you get strong and teach you how to protect yourself, you have to promise me that you won't go after these kids."

I smiled and said, "I can't promise you that."

"You're going to get strong, but if you hurt these kids it's going to be my fault, so you have to be responsible."

I promised, and he agreed to train me. He later joked, "Marc, you'll be a lot bigger than Everett Sinderoff."

Even though Everett looked like a Herculean figure in the poster, it turned out he was only 5'7" and weighed 150 pounds. I was already bigger.

The Boys & Girls Club weight room was old school. They had one bench, one squat rack, a small rack of dumbbells, and one pull-up bar. At first, I could only hang on that bar but it would soon become my mission to be a pro at pull-ups. The bars were old and the plates were rusty. Some of the 45-pound weights actually weighed 43½ pounds.

After that first workout at the Boys & Girls Club, I was so exhausted that I thought I was going to die. My grandfather called me the next day to ask why I wasn't in the gym.

I said, "I have to do that every day?"

I was starting to understand the amount of work it took not just to be an athlete but to play sports and be better than everyone else. It didn't take long before I was committed and pretty soon the weight room became my favorite place. Technically, I wasn't allowed to be in there until I was 14 but I learned how to sneak in the back door. I'm not even sure they knew I was there. Eventually, Abe bought me my first gym membership by paying $30 for the entire year.

Guys would come and go from that gym but I'd train for hours. I was often the only person there. It was my sanctuary and an outlet where I could release all my frustrations. I always tried to lift more weight. I liked the feeling of being spent and the blood pumping up my muscles. I wanted to get bigger, stronger, and more fit. I felt so much fear every day that it became the motivation I needed to build myself up and do something about it. I never wanted to feel like I did that day on the basketball court ever again. Pretty soon, I didn't need that motivation. I went to the gym because I had come to love it.

I bounced around from one gym to the next, but after working out inside the Durfee High School weight room, I asked my mom for a real gym membership. Not to just any gym but to the best gym in Fall River: Bodybuilding Plus. The gym was in the old Fall River Mills building. At 60,000 square feet, it was the mecca for serious training in my area. Many members were bodybuilders and local athletes, and it had all the best equipment, including four racks of dumbbells between five and 180 pounds.

I had no business asking my mom for such a costly gift. Putting her on the spot was unfair. We didn't have the money, but my mom leaned over to me, looked me in the eyes, and asked me if I really wanted this.

"Yes! Yes! Absolutely!" I said.

She explained how rent, utilities, and gas for the car left us with very little money for groceries. She pulled out four $20 bills and told me this was what she had set aside for groceries that month. I felt like a knucklehead and told her that I could keep going to the Boys & Girls Club. A few weeks later, my mom picked me up from school and drove me to Fall River Mills. She asked me if I wanted to check out Bodybuilding Plus. I couldn't have been more excited.

We walked over to the front desk and were greeted by a young woman named Lisa Swidney. Lisa was an incredibly athletic-looking young woman. My mom asked about the policy for kids and was told anyone under 16 could sign up with their parent's consent.

My mom asked me one more time, "Is this what you really want?"

"Absolutely!" I yelled. "I'll get in the best shape of my life!"

She pulled out an envelope containing $100 in cash and bought me a one-year membership. It was a sign from God. I knew this was going to put me in a position to train and get ready to play sports.

Lisa was my first trainer. She gave me a basic program of three days per week and spent hours helping me find my way around the gym. On the off days, I would do cardio or something to increase my base of conditioning.

Once I was on my own, my first workout partner was another 13-year-old, a Portuguese kid named Paul Coluro. He was already a big kid who really enjoyed training, and we hit it off. One day, Paul brought a bottle of Joe Weider's Chewable Amino Acids. We read the back of the bottle, which said to consume 28 pills before working out to increase muscle growth. We looked at each other as if to say, "Who's going first?" I popped six in my hand, threw them in my mouth, and started to chew these huge horse pills. I would chew six, then guzzle some water and repeat. They tasted like vanilla-flavored chalk. Then Paul would take some pills. I burped and white dust flew out of my mouth. I didn't take them again.

We would train for one or two hours and then walk to a Portuguese bar across the street to meet his dad. The place was tiny, but there were about 100 shit-faced Portuguese construction workers packed into a bar that was supposed to hold 30. Sometimes, we would sit at a table drinking Mountain Dew until Paul's dad finished his drinks. My mom would've flipped had she seen me in that bar. The last thing in the world I wanted to lose was gym privileges so I made an executive decision to keep that to myself.

I went to the gym all the time. I didn't miss one day. I religiously followed my program and recorded my progress. Lots of the members got a kick out of me asking if I could work out with them. I got help and tips from everyone. I was fortunate to be around some great people who really looked out for me.

When you set out to do something that's important to you, it's interesting how people come out of the woodwork to help you reach your goal. I don't believe in self-made men. We all get lots of help along the way, sometimes without even realizing it.

A couple months later, Richie Dias at the gym started calling me "D1." I didn't know what that meant. I didn't care. I just liked being recognized. Richie had graduated from Durfee. He was a tall, athletic guy who always gave me a high five when I saw him.

"Do you know what "D1" stands for?" Richie asked.

"No, I don't."

"It's Division 1. Someday you'll play football at the highest level because you're paying your dues now and putting in so much time and effort."

When he said that, I felt good about myself. It gave me a boost of confidence. I guess he was right. I didn't see any other kids working out in the gym, at least no kids my age. Because of Richie's encouragement, I set my sights on playing for a Division 1 college football team. That was my goal, and I became fanatical about my workouts. During school, I stared at the clock waiting for the day to be over. As soon as 2:00 p.m. rolled around, I slung my backpack over my shoulder, bolted out of class, and walked to the gym in the old Mills building. Being in that weight room was the greatest feeling in the world, and it would become my obsession for years.

WHAT I LEARNED

Use your pain as fuel. Sometimes that can be the best motivation. I loved sports and wanted to play sports, but I was significantly overweight and lacking in confidence. Bullying made everything worse, but I found a way to turn that negative into the spark that inspired change.

CHAPTER 3

THE START OF FOOTBALL

"They told me I was different. Best compliment ever."

In middle school, my teachers told my mother that they wanted to put me in remedial classes. I was creative and learned things differently, which made me incredibly insecure about academics. I felt like an embarrassment to my mom but she wasn't having any of it. She told me that I would be fine and then marched into Morton Middle School to tell my principal that I would remain in the current curriculum. The teachers would have to do their job to help me when I needed it.

Some teachers ignored me while others spent hours helping me learn the simplest of lessons. I continued to struggle in school but I always maintained a B average. I would take my work home, sit down at the kitchen table, and grind it out. Part of the problem was that I wasn't interested in the subject matter, but I worked hard because I didn't want to let my mother down. I watched how hard she worked to support me and my brother and it made me want to do better. I wasn't doing it for me.

What I loved was football. That's where my head was at, but I was still too heavy to compete in the Fall River Pop Warner league, so my mother drove me several miles to Swansea to play in their youth system.

Watching football was one thing. Playing it was another. I was so nervous when I started out and began to dread going to practice because every practice started with a lap around the field. Running was not my thing. It felt like I was going to die every step of the way. Once we finished the lap, we would run through the classic Oklahoma drill: A ball carrier and a defender lined up facing each other several yards apart and then ran full steam right at each other. I was scared out of my mind the first time we did this drill. As the defender, I took a beating so many times that I started to get angry. Finally, I just ran right through the ball carrier. My coach jumped up and started hugging me. I immediately craved that acceptance and knew that if I could knock the shit out of the other kid, I would get that same praise.

I don't know if I liked the hitting part or if it was the encouragement I was addicted to, but from that moment forward, I was hooked. I played in Swansea for three years, and I started to get better at football while I fell in love with the game.

Around that same time, an older woman lived in our neighborhood at President Village. She befriended our family and regularly offered to help out my mother. One day, she saw me with my nose buried in a football magazine and was curious why that particular magazine captured my attention. I told her that all the athletes looked like superheroes and that I wanted to look like them someday.

It turns out the woman worked at a factory that sorted thousands of magazines for distribution. The next day, I heard a loud bang on the back door. I ran downstairs and saw that she had dumped a giant pile of sports magazines in between the screen and the wood door. *Sports Illustrated*, *Sporting News College Football Preview*, *NFL Football Preview*. You name it and it was there.

I felt like I won the lottery. I threw the magazines into a trash bag and rushed up to my room to soak in all the pictures and articles. I not only read every word but I studied those magazines. I knew the players' heights and weights, and I slowly began to realize the difference between an average player and an All-Pro. For some reason, I gravitated toward the defensive players: Lawrence Taylor, Andre Tippett, Reggie White, Derrick Thomas, and Ronnie Lott. Those players became my idols, and I studied them daily. Other kids locked themselves in their room to salivate over hand-me-down nudie magazines but there I was hoarding sports magazines. That was the beginning of my obsession.

I ripped out pictures and plastered them over my entire wall. Pretty soon, you couldn't even tell what color the wall was painted. I didn't realize it at the time but I had created what was known as a vision board. Those pictures were the first thing I saw in the morning and the last thing I saw before I went to bed. All I could think about was becoming one of those elite athletes, and I spent lots of time envisioning myself in each position and making incredible plays in my head. I made a promise to myself that I was going to be listed as an All-American in *College Football Preview*. To do that, I knew that I needed to be 6'2" and 230 pounds by my senior year of high school.

Around the time I began making it a daily ritual to visualize greatness, my Aunt Theresa gave us an awesome new machine called a VCR. I'll never forget the day we got it. That thing was amazing. You popped in a tape and watched anything from movies to sports. My mom had a friend with a huge collection of tapes who would let us pick out anything we wanted. I chose half movies, half sports. I memorized the lines to each movie and watched the sport tapes over and over again.

If it was a football video, I could tell you the play that was going to happen, the ball carrier, and who would make the tackle. I'm sure that was the early stages of my OCD, and I really picked up on the details. I noticed how the running back carried the ball when he was running in a certain direction. I'd see how the defensive players tried to knock out the ball from behind to cause a fumble. I even took note of the celebration dances. Just like with the magazines, I was always interested in the defensive players. I worshipped those guys. I couldn't wait to play high school football.

I had planned to go to the same high school as my brother, but Mike went to Diman Regional Vocational High to learn electricity as a trade. I didn't like the trades and Diman didn't have a football team. Even though I wanted to be just like my brother, I also knew that if I wanted any future in sports, I'd have to go to public school at Durfee. The high school was huge with thousands of students and awesome facilities. The first time I walked into the building, I was awed by the grandiose ceilings. The school also had a great football team so I decided that I would follow my own path and go there.

The summer before my freshman year, I attended what we called captain's practice. The practice was organized by the head coach but run by the team's captains in the high school gymnasium from 5:00 to 7:00 p.m. on Tuesdays and Thursdays.

My mother was so happy that I wanted to participate that she made sure I got there an hour early. She called it a respect thing. She would always say, "Value other people's time and they'll value your time." I thought that was a bit extreme but there was no negotiating with my mom, so I walked up to the field house at 4:00 p.m. on a hot Tuesday afternoon and anxiously waited for one of my future teammates to arrive.

A black Chevy Trailblazer pulled into the lot, and a guy stepped out with a military haircut wearing black Ray Bans. I couldn't tell if he was a senior or a coach. He walked up to the field house carrying two official regulation high school footballs.

"What's your name?" he asked.

I stuck out my chest, lifted my chin, and said, "Marc Megna!"

"Always shake a person's hand with a firm grip and look them in the eye."

For a second, I was pissed he said that to me but then I realized he actually cared. That made me appreciate the tip.

"My name is Bob Bogan, and I'm the new high school football coach."

I liked Coach Bogan instantly. He was only 25 years old, but his goal was to be a college coach and he felt high school was a great starting point. I didn't know much about coaching but I knew that he cared, and to me, that was everything.

"Who's your favorite NFL team, Marc?"

"The Patriots!"

"Favorite position?"

"Linebacker!"

"Favorite player?"

"Andre Tippett!"

"Are you in shape?"

"Yes, sir!"

"We'll find that out."

That made me nervous. For the past year, I had been eating healthier and playing sports all day. Between baseball, basketball, and working out to get ready for football, I was starting to wither away. I had grown from 5'6" and

196 pounds to 5'10" and 155 pounds, but I still had lots of work to do with my strength and conditioning.

Slowly, the rest of the kids began to trickle into practice. Tall, short, skinny, and fat—we ran the gamut. We had lots of Portuguese kids on the team, and some of the kids had full beards at 14. Coach Bogan didn't care what they looked like; it pissed him off that so many kids arrived after 5:00 p.m. Finally, we began a static group stretch inside the field house. The place smelled like stale sweat. Next came the moment in practice that I always feared—running. Coach Bogan lined everyone up at the starting line. He set his stopwatch for 12 minutes, blew the whistle, and we took off around the small indoor track.

I had a sophisticated strategy when I ran—I put my head down, pumped my arms, and ran like hell! I wanted to make it look easy and did my best impression of an Olympic track star, but by no means was it easy. I knew nothing about running mechanics, but I did know two things. First, I'd rather die than have anyone pass me. Second, I didn't want to look slow.

It felt like I belonged in that environment. After all, it was in my blood. My dad was a Durfee athlete. My Grandpa Abe was elected to the Durfee Hall of Fame. He was even the official scorer and statistician for the varsity basketball team for more than 30 years.

I used to come to the same field house with my Grandpa Abe to watch games. He would tell me all about the rich history of Durfee sports, and he knew everything. More importantly, he would preach the importance of hard work, discipline, and team cohesion. We must have gone to more than 100 Durfee games together.

Red and black championship banners lined the walls. They dated back decades and kept me motivated while some of the other guys slowed down or dropped out altogether. Coach screamed at the kids to pick up the tempo. I couldn't believe the things he said to motivate the kids.

"Run faster, you fat bastard!"

"Work off all that, Chourico!"

"You should stop shoving donuts in your mouth and exercise more! Maybe you can lose some of that jelly!"

It was all in good fun but I hated when the coaches hammered the other kids. I certainly didn't want to get singled out because I was lazy. I didn't have much in my gas tank but I made sure to use it all. At first, I just tried to catch the guy in front of me. Once I did that, I tried to catch the next guy. I quickly developed a reputation as a hard worker. I liked people recognizing my work ethic. That was a label I didn't mind.

After the run, some kids got sick and sat off to the side. The rest of us went into the weight room, a place I knew well. The Durfee High weight room was small and it didn't have much equipment. What they did have was rusty and outdated but I liked it just the same. One bench press, one squat rack, a Nautilus machine in the center, and a few extra bars. That was it. The floor was hard as hell and the walls were plastered with anatomy posters and pullouts from *Muscle & Fitness* magazine.

The coaches would get excited when they saw someone throwing around an impressive amount of weight. I wanted to lift heavy but I lost some strength after my weight loss. I always dreamed of having a superhero body and crazy athletic ability. So far, I was 0-2 on that front. Still, I was determined to make it on another level, athletically and physically, so I did whatever I could to get an edge. I loaded my backpack with books every day, even if I didn't need them, using it as a weight vest and hauling it around school. When I finally put it down at the end of the day, I felt light as a feather. I looked at every free moment as an opportunity to train. If I were home, I would make bets with myself to see how many push-ups I could crank out in an hour, and I would do sit-ups and crunches while my family watched TV.

For the first couple of weeks of captain's practice, Coach Bogan would look surprised to see me waiting at the field house when he arrived, but it quickly became routine. I showed up early and coach would give me some feedback by telling me what I should focus on that day. I kept showing up early because I wasn't going to miss an opportunity to get some extra instruction. It was only captain's practice and I'm pretty sure that he wasn't supposed to be there but he didn't care. Like me, he was a dreamer. He wanted to lead Durfee back to glory on the gridiron. Since he was young and had lots of energy, he was the perfect man for the job. I definitely did not want to let him down.

Before my freshman year, I made a list of three goals and posted them on the wall next to my bed. I would stare at that list every morning when I woke up and every night when I went to bed.

1. HAVE A WINNING SEASON
2. EARN THE RESPECT OF MY TEAMMATES
3. START AT LINEBACKER

It was most important to me that we did well as a team. Next, I wanted to play well and hopefully attract the attention of college programs.

Until high school, I had planned to join the military. I always thought my father's service in the military was admirable. My grandfather served in the US Army and was active during World War II. Several of my uncles served in the Navy. During family gatherings, Uncle Herb and Uncle Gus would share stories while they played cards. They smoked lots of cigarettes and had naval tattoos on their forearms. I also learned about the military through comic books and movies about Vietnam. These weren't the most credible sources but that's what I knew. My granddad was big on movies and he took me to see both *Full Metal Jacket* and *Platoon*, probably not a good idea since I was only 11. Watching a disgruntled Gomer Pyle blow his brains out gave me nightmares for weeks but I liked those movies just the same.

I had a Type-A personality and gravitated toward military culture, but once I got to high school, I looked at football as a new and better opportunity. I wanted to earn a scholarship and play in college. If I were going to fulfill that dream and accomplish my goal, I would have to accelerate the process.

WHAT I LEARNED

You choose your goals. You determine how much effort you give. You are in control of your attitude. And you are responsible for your actions. Your decisions and your habits shape your future. I was never the best athlete, but at a young age, I made a conscious decision to outwork everyone else and be the most conditioned player on the field. I found a way to compensate for my shortcomings. Those habits, and the mindset I developed at a young age, helped me every step of the way as my career progressed.

CHAPTER 4

HIGH SCHOOL

"Run around like a crazy person, and always give a great effort."

—Marc Megna

On my first day at Durfee High, I tried to get to school as early as possible to avoid any unnecessary social contact.

I was pigeon-toed as a kid and had terrible posture. Dr. LeMaire always told me to stand up straight and turn my feet outward when I walked. Kids would tease me constantly so I spent lots of time trying to teach myself to correct my walk. On the way to Durfee in the morning, I would force myself to straddle the line etched in the sidewalk. I'd always be the first one in homeroom so I'd sit and read *Sports Illustrated* until the other kids arrived.

I was shy, awkward, and self-conscious, but I wasn't completely alone. Jeff Caron, Peter "Sunny" Suneson, and Chris Herren became my close friends. Jeff was a great athlete with a short, military-style haircut who couldn't wait to play basketball for Durfee. We used to lift weights in his garage and pushed ourselves pretty hard. He also came from a great family. His parents were blue-collar folks who set a high standard for him.

Sunny was being raised by a single mom, just like me. Ms. Suneson was a nurse who worked hard to provide for her three kids. We used to hang out in his basement, which became known as "the speakeasy." We'd go there to talk sports and goof off. Ms. Suneson worked a lot so it was the perfect spot for us. Though she never checked on us, I'm convinced that she knew what went on in that basement. Chris Herren was by far the best athlete in the group, and he was already being groomed to be Durfee High's next basketball star. His dad was a state representative, and he had a huge house, so I loved going over there to hang out.

We also had our share of bad habits. We saw the older kids drinking beer so we drank beer. I hated the taste so I would crack open a can, take a sip, and try to make it last for hours so nobody would give me a hard time.

One thing everyone also did was chew tobacco. I didn't mind chewing tobacco, and wasn't smart enough at the time to understand the damage it could do, so I chewed along with the rest of the crew. We did it all. Dip consisted of Skoal and Copenhagen. Chew options were Beech-Nut and Red Man. Some kids would put a dip between their gums and lower lip while they also had a wad of tobacco leaves in the back of their jaw. A tin of tobacco was supposed to last a few days but ours would be gone by the middle of the day. It was like we were trying to see who could get mouth cancer first, but at the time, we thought we were officially men. You could always tell who had tobacco by the faded circle on the back pocket of their jeans. That's why you had to be careful what hallway you walked down in school. One wrong turn and you could lose your entire stash. Your closest friends were always trying to bum a dip.

Things changed the day someone added a joint to the mix. I was nervous. Drugs made me uncomfortable. I saw how my father acted when he smoked marijuana and used cocaine. I didn't want to be like that, but these guys were my friends and I wanted to belong. I used every excuse in the book to avoid smoking but I felt a lot of pressure and eventually was asked to buy marijuana for the group. "Screw you guys!" is what I should have said, but I had a better idea.

It hit me like a bolt of lightning. All I had to do was give them a rolled joint. Would those amateurs really be able to tell what was in it? I went through our spice cabinet and came across a bag of oregano. It looked just like pot...sort of. I added some other harsh spices to curb the odor. Now I had to roll a joint. That was easier said than done because I had no idea how to do it. It took me 20 tries to get it right but I finally accomplished the task. I rolled two and burned one to see if the smell was a dead giveaway. The other spices seemed to give it a strong, harsh scent. I just hoped that nobody would pick up on it.

I produced my first official joint to the group and got props for the efficient roll. We lit it up. The first kid took a hit and started coughing.

"Holy shit, Megs! Where the hell did you get this shit?"

"The kid a few apartments over," I said.

"It's strong as hell."

I let out a huge sigh of relief. It felt like I dodged a bullet, but kids still gave me shit for not smoking. Some would even say, "I'm not smoking if Megs is in the room." I guess it made them feel bad, but some of them confided in me that they didn't want to smoke either. I hated getting heckled, but I didn't want to become my father. That's what gave me the strength to turn them down every time.

My mother always told me that drugs would keep me from achieving my goals, and if someone was doing something I wasn't comfortable with, I didn't have to take part in it. More than anything, I didn't want to let my mom down. I knew how hard she worked so I didn't want to screw up. At high school parties, I somehow managed to say "no" to every joint and pill I was offered.

I wasn't a high school freshman long before it became clear that I had a serious problem in the classroom. I struggled with grammar and math. Every day, I had a full-blown panic attack about math class. I liked going to school but I had trouble focusing and was easily distracted. My mind was on sports. I'd daydream about practice or the upcoming game. I also had grown taller and shed a lot of weight so I started to receive attention from girls who previously ignored me. That distracted me even more. When I was called out for not paying attention, I responded by becoming the class clown and was often sent to the principal's office.

One day, I was stopped by the assistant principal, Vincent Fitzgerald. Mr. Fitz had worked in the school department for more than 30 years. He was chubby with white hair and pink skin and looked pure Irish. He always reeked of coffee and cigarettes, and his tinted, Coke-bottle reading glasses

Grandpa Abe had so much Durfee pride, right down to the tie.

Sunny and Chris on graduation day.

Football camp in New York after training hard in the off-season.

made him look like a cartoon character. He had seen me in the office several times, but he thought I had potential so he pulled me aside.

"Why are you such a disturbance?"

"There's no excuse," I told him.

"If I see you getting into any more trouble, I'm going to put my foot in your ass."

That was comical coming from a chubby, little man like Mr. Fitz, but I appreciated the fact that he cared enough to set me straight. I didn't know it at the time but Mr. Fitz would turn out to be a significant influence in my life and the father figure that I never had.

I made sure to behave in school but I fell even further behind. I had no idea what I was doing. Mrs. Powers, my algebra teacher, suggested I come to school early to get extra help and extra time. Extra time! That was exactly what I needed. When I learned something, I knew it cold, but it took me longer than most kids because I was a tactile learner. I was the turtle, not the rabbit. I needed someone to walk me through the steps on paper. I then had to take a mental picture of the process and file it away.

A group of teachers saw that several of their students were struggling with the curriculum and started a before-school program called Math Lab. They would arrive early and donate their time without extra compensation. It was an incredible act of kindness that I will never forget. Without their help, I never would have passed my math classes. I gladly woke up early and walked to school in the dark to get extra help, waiting outside the Math Lab class for Mrs. Powell. The other teachers looked half asleep but Mrs. Powell was always chipper. I pulled my desk to the front, and she'd walk me through the steps of each problem. Whenever I got frustrated, she'd tell me to calm down and take a deep breath. I felt stupid, but Mrs. Powell made me understand that I was just as smart as everyone else. I just had to learn differently. At first, I was ashamed that I had to attend the Math Lab. I didn't want the other kids to know, but once my grades started to improve, all I cared about were my test scores.

It felt good to do well in the classroom, but nothing was more exhilarating than the idea of wearing those Durfee colors out on the football field. That's what I had been dreaming about since grade school but I still had to earn my way. I wanted to play varsity right away but Coach Bogan separated the freshman from the upperclassmen. I had watched hundreds of hours of football but I didn't know the first thing about alignments or plays. I had lots to learn, and the freshman team was the perfect place for me to get my crash course in Football 101.

The freshman football coach was a man by the name of Jackie Doyle. He was a little man who had a goofy way about him with a head of hair that was always sticking out all over, but he had an athletic frame, and you could tell that he took great joy in coaching. After getting fitted for our equipment, he asked us what position we wanted to play and then we competed for those spots. If you could catch, they put you at receiver. If you were tall and could catch, they made you a tight-end. I was a big kid, so I went where all the other big kids went—the line. I hated playing in the line, but we didn't have any other big kids and I was out of luck. So be it. I looked at it as an opportunity to hit people.

When it came time for hitting drills, Coach Doyle lined up two of us five yards apart. One guy had the ball and the other guy had to make the tackle. I had done versions of that drill before in youth leagues, but I still had no idea how to hit so I just ran as fast as I could and tried to kill the kid with the ball. Coach Doyle liked how I threw my body into the ball carrier and moved me to linebacker. I was pumped! That was exactly what I wanted. Growing up, I watched Dick Butkus, Mike Singletary, and Junior Seau hammer their opponents, and it made me want to be just like them.

Inside linebacker became my spot. Whenever it came time to work on defensive drills, I would get chills. Every time I lined up, I could feel myself getting better. Coach Doyle would give me the signals to relay to the guys in the huddle. It was awesome! I'd call the play, line up, and then hit anything that moved. It was the best feeling. Over time, I learned to watch the movement of the offensive guards and have them lead me right to the ball carrier. Making plays was like a drug and I couldn't get enough.

I became a sponge. I wanted to learn everything and started to understand the nuances of the game. I figured out that high school linemen gave everything away. Right before the snap, if I saw a lineman raise his heels and put all his weight on his hand in front of him, I knew that a run was coming.

If a lineman was sitting back on his heels, I knew it was a pass or a pulling scheme.

In my very first freshman football game, I noticed how the running back would often give away where he was going. Before the snap, he would peek in the direction he was headed. I couldn't believe it. Just by looking around and picking up on these little clues, it felt like I was in the offensive huddle and already knew the play. I could start sprinting right before the ball was snapped. Getting a running start on a ball carrier taking a handoff is about as unfair as it sounds. After my first sack, I jumped up and pumped my fists in the air like the NFL players. I felt like Lawrence Taylor out there.

Freshman games were held on Friday afternoons after school. If it were a home game, we would play on our main field. The varsity team had a short practice and came to watch our game. Coach Bogan would attend as well. It wasn't common for freshman to play in varsity games, but Coach Bogan was different. He didn't give a shit what anyone thought. He was changing the culture and letting everyone know that the best players would play. I wanted to play varsity but to do that I needed him to see me dominate on the freshman team.

Brockton High School was a Massachusetts powerhouse. All their kids were big and athletic. I knew that game was my chance to stand out so I made sure to follow my pre-snap read progression. I went all out on every play and teed off on anyone in my way. It didn't go unnoticed. After the game, the varsity guys came up to me and told me I played well. I was one of three players Coach Bogan pulled aside and told to suit up for varsity the next day against Brockton. I was so excited! I had worked hard to get there and everything was coming together. I couldn't wait to get home and tell my mom, but she wasn't surprised, saying, "I knew you would play varsity. It was only a matter of time." I went to bed that night dreaming about the game the next day.

I became meticulous about my game day rituals. I woke up early Saturday morning and had a light breakfast. I packed my bag and made it over to the field house incredibly early to find Coach Bogan laying out the uniforms in the locker room. He tossed me a jersey. It was #49. Not the number I would have picked but I finally got the chance to wear the Durfee red and black. Coach told me that I would get to play special teams. When the rest of the team finally showed up, I put on my pads and went out to the field for warm-ups. In high school, pre-game takes forever. I was aching for the game to start.

When the captains from both teams walked to the middle of the field for the coin toss, I was in awe. I had never seen athletes that big in real life before. Brockton won the coin toss and deferred until the second half. That meant we received the ball at the start of the game and I'd be on the field for the kickoff.

When the ball was kicked toward us, I sprinted into place and turned around to search for my blocking assignments. The guy I was supposed to block looked like a missile aimed to kill me as he sprinted down the field. I took three steps and drove my helmet right above his knee. He went flying over my head. It was him or me and my man didn't make the tackle. That was all I cared about. He got up and immediately started screaming. "Fuck you! I'm gonna kill you, bitch!" The referee pulled him away, and I ran to the sidelines.

I felt like I got off to a good start, but the rest of the game was a mess. It seemed like Brockton scored every time they touched the ball. I got hammered out there on special teams, and that kid I blocked earlier lit me up. Our team got killed and I got my butt kicked. I was pissed because it looked like we gave up out there. I didn't want to show my face after the game. When I got home, I went straight to my room and shut the door. My mom came up to my room that night. She had a gift for being supportive when I needed it most.

"The score doesn't matter, Marc," she said. "The only thing that matters is your effort."

The winter after my freshman season, I started another ritual. This one was inspired by the movie *Rocky* and Sylvester Stallone's daily run through the streets of Philadelphia. Of course, if it was good enough for Rocky then it was good enough for me. I truly believed that it was necessary. My mother was perplexed.

"When are you doing this? Before school?"

"Yes, at 4:45 a.m.," I said.

"Marc, it's way too cold out there for you to be running through the streets."

"I'll be okay. I promise. It's important to be conditioned so I can have an edge when I play."

"You better be careful out there," she said. "If it's too cold, come back in. Promise?"

"Yeah. I promise."

The weather didn't matter to me. The night before, I laid out workout clothes on my bureau and made sure everything was in the exact order that I would put it on so I wouldn't waste any time: Undershirt, jogging pants, T-shirt, sweatshirt number one, and then sweatshirt number two. I needed two sweatshirts because it was freezing. The last item was an extra thick pair of socks and a winter skull cap. No gloves. That's right. At the time, I was too much of a tough guy to wear mittens.

I was so excited that it was difficult to sleep the night before. I'd toss and turn, thinking about the path for my morning run. I'd start by jogging over to the high school for a warm-up, run my sprints on the track, and then take it back home.

That first day, my alarm sounded at 4:45 a.m. and I sprung out of bed. Having been inspired by the sense of urgency displayed by soldiers in military movies, I dressed as quickly as possible and bolted out the front door. I don't know what the temperature was that first morning, but it was cold. Extremely cold! The piercing wind hit me in the face. Naturally, it had snowed overnight so there was a slick layer of powder covering the streets. I put that out of my mind and trudged down the road. No warm-up, just a slow jog. I wasn't around the first corner before I questioned how long I would last. It also became immediately clear that I would need gloves next time. I pulled my sweatshirt over my hands and gripped the cuffs of my sleeves when I ran to prevent my hands from growing numb.

I reached the high school, hopped the fence, and ran down the hill toward the track to run my sprints. I crept past the security guard sleeping in his patrol car and arrived to see that the track also was covered with snow. Since I was already there, I decided to finish my work out on the slippery surface. No turning back now. Slipping and sliding, I ran my 80s, 60s, and 40s. I managed to get them all in and fell only once. When I finished, I made a habit of walking over to the giant rock dedicated to a Durfee alumnus by the name of Malcolm "Mac" Aldrich. I put my hand on the rock and thought about what I had just done and what I wanted to accomplish in the future. After that, in my loudest scream to celebrate completion of the workout, I would let out a giant, "Yeah!"

I wasn't done yet. I hit the timer and ran home as fast as possible. I cut through yards and driveways to save time. Once I made it back to my front door, I threw my hands in the air and smiled. I don't know what compelled me to make that final run. It wasn't part of the plan, but that short sprint back to my house made me push myself to compete against my previous time. Waking up early to get in a challenging workout became a tradition that I've held onto for almost three decades.

In the book, *Outliers*, author Malcolm Gladwell says that it takes roughly 10,000 hours of practice to achieve mastery in any field. Gladwell studied the lives of extremely successful people to find out how they achieved success. I never was the best athlete but because of workouts like the ones I started doing in high school, I got my conditioning to such a high level that I was not only able to compete but thrive. While my peers faded, I got stronger. I could go harder and longer. I rarely got tired or changed my tempo. I could perform at the same pace and the same level from the start of practice to the end. It took me years to get to the level where I broadened my aerobic base and developed my anaerobic capacity where I could keep going, but once I did, I felt like the Energizer Bunny.

Conditioning had to be a nonfactor. If I was fatigued, I couldn't practice the sport-specific components of football and at that point, I had a lot to learn. On a skill level, I wasn't there yet but I was beginning to make progress because of my commitment and consistency. When I look back over those videos of my freshman football games, I can see that I wasn't thinking only about making the tackle, I was trying to punch the ball loose at the same time. When battling with blockers, I was placing my hands inside so I could pull and push them around. I was starting to learn the game.

The summer before my sophomore year, I planned on attending as many football camps as possible. I enjoyed Marty Fine's Navy Prep Football Camp the most. It was held in Portsmouth, Rhode Island at the local high school field. All the kids were either from Durfee or Portsmouth. That camp was fun because I got to spend time with my teammates. It wasn't full contact. We wore only helmets and shoulder pads, but having another team there heightened the competition. Both teams got better. Portsmouth and Durfee couldn't have been more different. I respected the Portsmouth players; they were smart and fundamentally sound while the Durfee kids were tougher and hard-nosed. Things would get heated at times and a couple of players would occasionally go at it but nothing ever got out of hand.

One of the most popular football camps in the country was an offense/defense camp in Stony Brook, New York. The competition was great and that's where I realized that I could compete against anyone in the country. At the end of camp, they held a massive scrimmage and paired off kids based on skill level. They put me on the A team and we played the B team. I made several tackles and caused a fumble. The coach told me I had an outstanding game. The positive feedback I got from my fellow players built my confidence a great deal. I always felt that being recognized by your teammates was the ultimate compliment.

What also drew me to that camp was that NFL athletes would come out to coach and give daily speeches. That gave me the chance to meet some of my childhood heroes.

I convinced Sunny to attend with me and we drove up together. Once we got settled in our dorm and hit the cafeteria, we headed to the field for our first speech by an NFL player. Sunny and I took seats on the grass when we saw someone walk out. I didn't know who it was at first. I just saw a 6'4", 290-pound giant with no neck and Oakley sunglasses towering over me. It turned out he was three-time, All-Pro defensive tackle Leonard Marshall. He was a legend with three Super Bowl rings, and he was huge. I weighed 205 pounds and looked like one of his legs. I couldn't get over that a real-life, All-Pro defensive tackle was standing right in front of me.

Marshall talked about hard work and effort.

"Y'all may think we're working hard but you always have more to give," he said. "Bust your butts out there on that field!"

His speech got me excited. I was chomping at the bit to get going. The next morning, we started off with a traditional warmup and calisthenics. Practice was structured much like high school practice, including individual work and more position-specific drills. I loved it all and was having a blast. I don't know if it was a good thing to get so much joy out of smacking a ball carrier but I liked the feeling.

After lunch, a white Jaguar pulled up to the field. The windows were down and we could hear music blasting. It was our next speaker. When I saw a large gentleman get out of the car with an earring in the shape of the number 56, I couldn't believe my eyes. It was Lawrence Taylor of the New York Giants, one of the greatest defenders who ever lived and my all-time favorite player. I hated the Giants, but this was Taylor, a 6'4", 250-pound, hard-charging athletic monster. All the campers were in awe.

Taylor talked to us for 20 minutes about the joy of football and teamwork. After the speech, he took a few questions. A hundred kids raised their hands but for some odd reason, he picked me.

"Stand up little man. What's your question?"

I was so excited that I raised my hand without having a question. I just wanted to talk to Taylor and was so nervous that I blurted out the first thing that came to mind.

"Who do you think is the best player coming out of college this year for the NFL Draft?" I asked.

"Speak up, son. You talk like a girl."

Oh man, I was embarrassed. He just humiliated me in front of the entire camp. I didn't want to ask him that question again, but I cleared my throat, raised my voice, and repeated it loudly.

"Who do you think is the best player coming out of college this year for the NFL Draft?"

"That's better. I think the best player is that fast boy outta Notre Dame," Taylor said. "I hope his fast ass goes to the CFL so I don't have to chase him."

The player he was referring to was Raghib "Rocket" Ismail, a wide receiver at Notre Dame, my favorite college team, but I wasn't thinking about any of that. The whole incident irritated me. Taylor was my hero but he went from first to worst in seconds. I hated Taylor and the Giants from that day forward.

I always looked up to athletes and put them on a pedestal, but they were still people who put their pants on one leg at a time just like me. Some were cocky, some were arrogant, and some were incredibly humble. Character started to mean more to me than ability. That's what drew me to Andre Tippett of the New England Patriots. Andre was an incredible role model. He was humble, hardworking, and exceptionally kind. It always blew my mind how someone could be such an aggressive warrior on the field and then such a gentleman off the field. That was exactly who I wanted to be.

Thanksgiving Day Battle versus New Bedford High School

WHAT I LEARNED

Confidence is developed through preparation, experience, and repetition. Picture yourself being successful. Run through every possible scenario in your head so that when it's time for the real thing, you've been there before and can act on instinct.

CHAPTER 5

A CHANGE IN PERSPECTIVE

"I care less about your potential and more about what you do with it. The world has enough gifted underachievers."

—Donnell Boucher

Before my junior year, Mr. Fitz got me a job at the high school working in his office. I'd input data, sort paperwork, and get lunch for him.

"Marc, it's time," he'd say as he tapped his watch.

"Yes, sir."

Mr. Fitz ate like a truck driver on an episode of *Man vs. Food*, and fetching his lunch was the least I could do. He was very serious and ran the office like a military operation, and he liked only two things for lunch. It was either, "Get me a coffee malted frappe and two hot dogs with red pepper relish from Newport Creamery." Or he would say, "Get me just a coffee malted frappe. My stomach is a bit upset." That was no surprise since his "breakfast of champions" consisted of two jelly donuts and a large glass of milk.

He'd grab his walkie-talkie to call the on-duty security guard to give me a ride to Newport Creamery, "Two to base. I repeat two to base." If there was a long pause, it usually meant the guard was sound asleep, but he'd eventually come to pick me up at the cafeteria entrance and off to Newport Creamery we went.

I spent lots of time with Mr. Fitz that summer. He became a part of my support system and always was there when I needed help. He'd take me to the movies or buy me something to eat when my mother was working. He knew Fall River so when he saw me with troubled kids, he'd pull me aside. I would not be where I am today if I hadn't met him.

One afternoon, I came back from the lunch errand to find my Grandpa Abe inside the office talking with Mr. Fitz. He shut the door and told me to sit down. My grandfather sat down next to me, looked me in the eyes, and told me that my dad had passed away that morning. At first, I smiled. I thought it was a joke. *How could he be gone?* He was only 49 years old and looked great the last time I saw him. When reality sunk in, I burst into tears and hugged my grandfather. All I could say was, "No, no, no…" over and over again.

"He was supposed to see me play football this year," I cried.

I hadn't seen my dad in eight months. He avoided spending time with me and my brother, and I had been determined to change that and become a part of his life again by becoming a great football player. That day in the principal's office, my grandfather told me that my dad would be at every game, watching from above.

I was a mess, but it was difficult to pinpoint why I was so upset. Why was I shedding so many tears for a person who wanted nothing to do with me? Was I upset because he was gone? Was it because I hadn't seen him in so long? Was it because he never saw me excel in any sport? Was it because I never got to have the father-son relationship I wanted so badly? Was it because the man who was my father, the man I loved so much, was gone? Maybe it was all of those reasons.

"Marc, go home and get some rest," said Mr. Fitz, giving me the rest of the day off. "I'm worried about you. If you need anything, give me a call."

Of course, I didn't go home. I went straight to the Fall River YMCA. Anger fueled me. I couldn't wrap my head around the fact that I'd never see my father again. I wasn't ready for that harsh reality. I trained for several hours that day, and my arms and legs hurt for days.

My mom usually waited for me down the street but that day was different. She came inside and waited for me. She hugged me and we walked out together. When we reached the sidewalk, she burst into tears. I started crying because my mom was crying.

I finally had to ask her, "Why are you crying? I thought you hated Dad."

"I know how much you wanted to spend time with your father. He's gone now and you won't be able to," she said. "He loved you, Marc. He just struggled with so many things. Don't ever forget that he loved you."

Hearing that really helped me. I think she saw all his flaws, but she knew he loved his kids and he did everything he could. Deep down, she knew he was a good person, but she realized some men just weren't meant to be dads. That was my mom. She always focused on the positive.

My dad died alone in his apartment and I'm convinced drugs played a role in his death. He pushed himself, drank lots of coffee, and smoked cigarettes. He rarely slept and wanted to squeeze every second out of every day. I don't know where he picked up his habits but I wish he had found other means to try and get ahead.

I've since committed my entire life to being fit and healthy. I believe in my heart that my dad would've liked the adult me. We definitely would've been close friends. If I had one wish, it would be to go back to that time so I could use my education and life experiences to help him. I know that I would have been able to turn him around. There's not one day that goes by that I don't think of my father. And when I think about his death, it upsets me. My mind races. I sweat. I get edgy and frustrated.

When my father passed away, I had a defining moment of clarity as I realized that the clock was ticking. I didn't want my own life to be ordinary so I pursued everything from school to training and football with intensity. I had a vision. I knew where I wanted to go and I headed down that road with a sense of urgency.

I also learned how to harness my anger, pain, and heartache and turn it into controlled aggression. I looked forward to hitting people on the field. It became my therapy and made me feel better about life and my problems. That newfound aggression also helped me take my training and conditioning up a notch. I may have been an average athlete but effort set me apart. When running wind sprints during practice, I would make sure to outwork the guy next to me. If we had to run 12 suicides, I might be beaten on the first two or three but I would always win the rest because everyone else faded. I had staying power that I could call upon when tired. When others let up on the gas, I went harder. It didn't matter if my chest felt like it was going to explode or if I was on the verge of passing out. I'd rather die than let anyone see me dogging it. That became my "It" factor.

During my first couple years at Durfee, I did everything by the book. On the football field, I wanted to please the coaching staff so I knew my assignments inside out. I knew where I was supposed to be and I would be there but something was missing. I didn't know what that something was until my junior year—specifically, during our game against Attleboro High. They were good and I quickly found out why. As soon as the game started, they jumped out to a big lead. They had a linebacker named Dave Menard who ran all over us. We were getting killed and it was embarrassing.

The game got so far out of reach that something just clicked inside me. I knew that I had no control over the score, but what I could control was the way I played. Suddenly, I didn't give a shit anymore. I didn't have to worry about making a mistake. That didn't mean I forgot my assignments, but I knew that one mistake wouldn't make a difference at that point. I didn't care that we were losing; I was going to kill myself on every down. I stopped looking at the scoreboard and focused on making as many plays as possible. No more conformity. No more systematic routine. I was a madman who threw my body around with reckless abandon. It started to work. I sacked the quarterback. I shredded a block and took down Menard behind the line of scrimmage for a loss. I wasn't just making tackles but I was also knocking out the ball. I was creating plays and being productive. With each play, my confidence grew. Now I was having fun. *Why haven't I been playing like this the whole time?*

We didn't come close to winning that game. I don't even know the final score, but when I walked off that field, I realized that before that game I had been playing scared. That's what was preventing me from making plays. Being where you're supposed to be on the field wasn't always the same as being where you needed to be to make an impact. I needed to go out there every game and do what I did against Attleboro. That's precisely what I did and that's what made me stand out.

From that day on, I didn't give a fuck. I no longer cared how I was perceived. I was still going to be a gentleman but I was going to do what I wanted to do. That game against Attleboro changed the way that I played football and people took notice.

A few weeks after the season ended, the All-Conference Team was selected. I felt like I was a lock to make the team, but when I read the newspaper the day it was announced, I was furious. I didn't make the team. Our conference was called The Big Three. There were only three freaking teams, and I wasn't even on the All-Conference Team. Coach Bogan was upset as well. He called me to the office that day and told me that I should have been on the team, but I knew that if I was good enough to be on that team then I would have been. That night I sat on the floor of my room and stared up at all the posters of college and pro athletes and realized that I was off course. If I was going to be good enough to play at the college level, I had to do better.

I immediately started mapping out a training plan for the off season. I needed more strength and a few extra pounds. Any edge I could get would be helpful going into my senior year. I took my conditioning up a notch, too. Whenever I ran, I kept going until it felt like I was sucking oxygen through a small straw. Rest would be minimal. I had to push myself to a point where I thought about giving up. That was the essential component. I needed to feel like I couldn't handle it anymore. Being able to push through that mental barrier was the actual drill.

The one problem I had with all the regular drills was they weren't actual game-type scenarios so I came up with a unique style of conditioning. I would put on my cleats, walk out to the field, and pretend that I was in an actual game. I played offense, defense, and special teams. I would start as if I was on offense and block my opponent then run downfield and block someone else. I'd pass block on the next play. I would run three to six plays like that and then simulate running 40 yards to cover a punt. Once on defense, I would make up every possible scenario. I'd tackle the ball carrier after a five-yard run. I'd get to the quarterback using my best pass rush move. I'd stop and change direction to chase down the ball carrier on a draw play. I was training for actual performance. Agility training and straightforward conditioning were excellent but nothing had the carryover effect like real play simulation.

During the summer, my good friend, Jeff Caron, let me borrow Strength Shoes to help my speed. The shoes were white and had a giant rubber platform underneath the front of the foot that kept your heel off the ground. The point was to keep your calf flexed so it was like doing a calf raise every step you took. I'm not sure how healthy it was for my ankle joint but I gave it a shot. Three days a week, I would take the shoes to an industrial area and set up shop in a vacant parking lot. I would leave my car radio on and do an hour of Strength Shoe work. My calves burned like no tomorrow.

Over the course of senior year, my stock started to rise, and I became a solid college football prospect. I made good on my promise to myself. Not only did I make the All-Conference Team but I was named an All-State linebacker by *The Boston Globe*, which was a big deal in Massachusetts. However, it still felt like I wasn't getting the credit I deserved because Durfee didn't do well. We didn't have a great season so the players at the powerhouse schools like Brockton and Xaverian Brothers were the ones thrust into the spotlight.

I had my sights set on the bigger picture. No one in my family had ever gone to college, but I wanted an opportunity to get a higher education and it also was important that I play football at the top level. Since I was young, I had pushed myself to overcome numerous obstacles, but college was intimidating. I knew it wouldn't be easy, but I was up for the challenge. I also realized that it wasn't just about me. I didn't want to let my mother down. She sacrificed so much and worked long hours to put food on the table. She'd come home exhausted from work and only had a few minutes to spend with us before she went right back out to work her second job. I didn't want to screw this up.

I wanted to attend a local college so that I could be close to my mother and my brother, and entertained the idea of attending one of the military academies. I appreciated the discipline and liked the structure. I even obtained the standard letter of recommendation from US Representative Barney Frank, but I was concerned about not being able to experience traditional college life. Several schools were talking to me, including Boston College, Northeastern University, and University of Massachusetts (UMass), but it was the University of Richmond who took an early interest in me and sent defensive coordinator Jim Reid for my first-ever recruiting visit.

I heard stories about these visits and didn't know what to expect. I lived in the Rolling Green apartment complex in the North End of Fall River and hoped Coach Reid wouldn't have any trouble finding our apartment. He called when he was a few minutes away and told me he was looking forward to meeting my mother. Of course, my mom had cleaned the apartment from top to bottom as she always did when we expected company.

Coach Reid rang the bell at the front of the complex and we buzzed him in. I told my mother that I hoped he entered the back lobby entrance since the front was dirty and the carpet torn up. No such luck. I opened the door and there he was, standing in the hall with a sports jacket and shoes shined to perfection. He was a fit man in his fifties and stood with military-like posture, his shoulders thrown back. He exuded an aura of confidence and positivity that I had never experienced before.

"Hello Marc, it's great to see you," he said with a huge grin.

"It's great to have you here, Coach."

He stuck his hand out, grabbed mine with a death grip, and pulled me off my feet. I think he was checking to see how strong I was on my feet. When he walked over to my mother, I was terrified that he would throw her across the room with that handshake because she only weighed 110 pounds, but he gave her the mini-version—a little pull, but not too much. Thank goodness because he could have done some damage.

My mom had a huge smile on her face.

"Hello, Coach Reid," she said. "It's nice to meet you."

Coach Reid took a seat on the couch next to my mother and me. He told us all about the program at Richmond and what life would be like for a student-athlete at the private, liberal arts university with more than 4,000 students. I was nervous about being away from home and going to college in the south. I didn't know how the students from that area would treat me, but he assured me that it wasn't an issue and said that Richmond had a lot of students from the New England area.

"Marc, you will not only get a degree at Richmond but you'll graduate with distinction," he said, looking my mother in the eye.

Most football programs want players to maintain only a 2.0 grade point average so they can remain eligible. Coach Reid wasn't a fan of the word "eligible." He thought athletes should maintain a 3.0 average, at the very least. He didn't want any of his players hanging on for dear life. He wanted them to excel academically. He promised that he would keep me focused and that I would get good grades.

Coach Reid made it sound like Richmond was the greatest place on earth. He described the dining hall and mentioned it being one of the top-ranked cafeterias. He had our mouths watering. It sounded like a five-star restaurant. I thought the entire university was like Disneyland. Both my mom and I sat there in awe. This was all very new to us. Nobody in my family went to college so we didn't know anything about campus life. My mom kept looking at me and smiling. She was so excited about the possibility of her son going to college. It looked like she was fighting back tears.

Coach Reid discussed the football program and how the staff closely monitored players during training and practice. He thought that I would fit their program perfectly. He looked at my mom and told her, "I believe your son will get a degree. I believe your son will be a captain. I believe your son will be an All-Conference player."

He liked the fact that I was a hard worker. He said that he only recruited men who were honest, responsible, and hardworking. I'll never forget that. Hearing somebody compliment me and believe in me gave me goosebumps and a jolt of energy. Up until that point, the way I lived and structured my life made others think I was obsessed. Maybe I was but Coach Reid appreciated my work ethic. He was the first person to make my obsession seem normal and essential when it came to achieving my end goal. I assumed that was the way Coach Reid talked to every recruit but years later he told me that it wasn't the standard talk. He told me a little more about his strategy.

"I have to be careful what I say and only say what I believe to be true," he said. "Marc, you have a certain thing known as charisma. You exude it. Charisma is how you carry yourself. Some people are born with a certain look. Some people look others in the eye instead of looking over their shoulder. You can always tell if people are committed by how they speak, how they look at you, and how they conduct themselves when you're talking with them. To me, commitment is your belief in a purpose."

He continued, "When you talked to me, Marc, you believed that you would be an outstanding player. A lot of people talk but seldom do I believe what they're saying. It's rare to find people who follow through. I guess what I'm trying to say is that it's rare that people back up their words."

If you talk the talk, then you must walk the walk. I admired him so much because that's how he lived his life. It was why he had bags under his eyes. He wasn't worried about who was going to win. That came down to hard work and ability. The most important thing to him was following through on the promises he had made to parents, especially mothers and grandmothers. He wanted to keep those promises and made a strong impression on me when we met. I trusted him. I didn't want to let him down. He eventually became another father figure to me and it started that night.

I've heard Coach Reid tell people the story about the night we met but his perspective is a bit different. He says that there was one thing that turned him off and it was that my goal was to become an NFL player. He didn't see an NFL body and he didn't see NFL speed. He saw a well-groomed kid who was 6'1" and 225 pounds. I wasn't pudgy, but I wasn't hard either so I had further to go with my training. Coach Reid didn't want to bring me to a school only to shatter my dreams but he had a point. To put it in perspective, I wasn't getting recruited by big Division 1 schools. Richmond was a small, 1-AA school that didn't have a history of sending players to the NFL. Coach Reid thought I was nuts but he liked my focus.

He did his homework on me. He liked the person he saw. He was told that I was polite, respectful, humble, and attended class so he decided to offer me a scholarship. Richmond was the only school that offered me a scholarship. Northeastern was interested but they only offered me a scholarship after Richmond did. It was clear how Coach Reid's recruiting eye carried some weight.

I visited Northeastern and liked it, especially since it was close to home. I also liked that my mom and brother could watch the games. At the end of my Northeastern visit, Head Coach Barry Gallup brought me into his office.

He shook my hand, pulled me in for a long hug, and said, "I think you know this school is for you."

It was awkward, even borderline scummy. For a while, I thought that I was going to Northeastern, but I liked Coach Reid. My mother loved Coach Reid.

I promised him I would visit and I had a blast. I loved the school and the campus and how everyone was so passionate about the program. I hadn't been anywhere that beautiful in my life, but that wasn't the real reason I wanted to go to Richmond. I was going there to play for Coach Reid. If he coached at the University of Alaska, I would've signed on to play there in a second. That's how powerful an impact Coach Reid made on me when we met. He also hit it off with my mother, who was fired up for days after his visit. He had a history of being able to talk with parents and be honest about what was going on with their sons. Still, I wasn't going to make my official decision until the Monday after I returned.

Back at school, I spotted Coach Gallup and a few other assistants from Northeastern walking into the main office at Durfee. *Holy shit! What the hell is he doing here?* I was shocked. Luckily, I bumped into Mr. Fitz. I had been in constant communication with him during my trip and he knew that I wanted to attend Richmond. He gave me a warning.

"They're looking for you and they want your decision," he said.

I made my way to the main office. I greeted Coach Gallup and the rest of the Northeastern staff. Mr. Fitz put us in a private office. They were all convinced that I was going to Northeastern so I was incredibly nervous. I was shaking, but I picked my head up, looked Coach Gallup straight in the eyes, and thanked him for recruiting me and the opportunity he presented.

"I've decided to go to the University of Richmond," I said. "I think it's the best place for me and I was very comfortable there."

"I'm disappointed, Marc," he said. "I think you're making a mistake, but I do wish you all the luck in the world. I hope things go well for you, except when you play us."

The next day, the staff at Northeastern sent a fax to the Durfee office. It was the depth chart of the players on the University of Richmond roster. There was a note attached: "The Richmond defense is loaded with freshman and sophomores at every position. You probably won't even get a chance to play there until your junior year."

That upset me and made me nervous at the same time, but I looked at it as another challenge. I knew nothing would be handed to me. The best players would play. It was up to me to go out and prove that I deserved to be on that field. Coach Bogan always told me, "Marc, you have to play the way you have always played. You have to play with that contagious energy and high motor. When you don't, you're just like everyone else."

I never forgot that statement. It stuck with me during my entire collegiate and professional career.

On signing day, Coach Bogan set up a small press conference at the high school for the local media. It was an amazing day. My mom, Abe White, and Mr. Fitz were there along with my friends, Chris, Jeff, and Peter. They were the people who supported and believed in me from day one. Coach Bogan spoke about my choice and how I wanted a first-class education to go along with the college football experience. Once again, my mom cried. Grandpa Abe hugged me and whispered to me in his most sarcastic voice, "Don't screw this up."

I was anxious to get out of Fall River and start college but I wasn't coasting. I had also made a commitment to keep pushing myself and to keep improving. I knew how much work it took for me to reach that point. I also knew that to perform at the next level, I not only had to keep my foot on the gas but I had to take it up a notch. I wasn't trying to be perfect. I wasn't trying to impress the coaches. Excelling at football wasn't my only goal. I wanted to evolve as a person. It was important to me to continue going to class, turn in my work on time, and make the most of my opportunity. I didn't want to talk about it or tell people what I was going to do. I was just going to do it and keep my mouth shut. That's the way that I was brought up.

One day in March, Coach Bogan pulled me out of class. That was unusual so I was nervous.

"Marc, I have some bad news," he told me. "Coach Reid is leaving Richmond. He took the defensive coordinator job at Boston College."

I couldn't believe it. Coach Jim Reid was the only coach I believed in and the only coach I trusted through the entire recruiting experience. The news crushed me. I was second guessing my decision to attend Richmond. Being 500 miles away from home seemed so much harder without him.

Coach Reid asked that I visit him at Boston College so he could explain the situation. Coach Bogan and I made the trip together to Chestnut Hill, which is about an hour north of Fall River. When we arrived at the athletic center, Coach Reid's enthusiasm made me temporarily forget about the current situation. We talked for a bit in his office and I understood why he left. It was an excellent situation for him. Boston was his hometown, there was a significant increase in pay, and it was an opportunity to coach a Division 1A defense.

He then showed me the Boston College team picture on the wall. "Do you know who these guys are, Marc?"

"Yes, sir. They are awesome football players." I had been watching them for years and knew how special they were.

"You're just as good as them," he said.

That was crazy to hear. I didn't believe it but that was Coach Reid. He was always pumping people up and letting them know what was possible. That's why I so badly wanted to play for him. He had this way of making you feel special and indestructible.

He walked us through the athletic facility. We saw the football field and weight room. I was in awe. I always wanted to go to Boston College. I had a brief glimmer of hope that Coach Reid would ask me to come with him. At one point, I even asked him if there was room for me on his team.

He smiled and said, "Richmond is the school for you, Marc. I think this will all work out. You never know what the future holds."

At the time, I didn't understand what he meant by that statement. I should've known that Coach Reid had a plan in his head. He was always thinking ten moves ahead of everyone else. In the meantime, I had to swallow a bitter pill.

WHAT I LEARNED

Don't take anything for granted. Life can change in a moment's notice. Each day is a gift, so no matter what you're doing, give it everything you have so that you don't have any regrets.

CHAPTER 6

THE UNIVERSITY OF RICHMOND

"There's no talent here. This is hard work. This is an obsession. Talent doesn't exist. We are all equals as human beings. You could be anyone if you put in the time. You will reach the top, and that's that. I'm not talented. I am obsessed."

—Conor McGregor, UFC featherweight champion

Nothing prepared me for the shock of being a student-athlete at the University of Richmond.

I had a rude awakening on my very first day. My mother had just dropped me off and I was sitting in my dorm room with two teammates, DJ Cunningham and Elio Imbornone. Elio was a fellow New Englander, whom I met on my recruiting trip to Richmond. The three of us were all so excited about our first day that we didn't realize that time had gotten away from us.

There was an aggressive knock on the door. We jumped up. I opened the door to find Defensive Line Coach Joe Cullen standing in the hall and he was mad as hell.

"Marc, what the hell are you doing?"

"Just talking with Elio and DJ, Coach."

"Do you three idiots know there's a goddamn team meeting happening right now?"

"No, sir. I thought it was at…"

"Get your asses over to the team room right now!"

As we started walking down the hall, Coach Cullen screamed, "Fucking run!"

We ran as fast as we could over to the meeting room. Once we got inside, Head Coach Jim Marshall gave us the look of death.

"After this meeting, I want Marc, Elio, and DJ to see Coach Cullen," he roared. "Men, never, ever, ever be late to anything while you're a Richmond student-athlete. If you can't be on time, then be early."

The program took a chance on me. Technically, they didn't need to recruit outside of Virginia because they had plenty of potential talent. I didn't want to mess up or do anything that would make me feel like any more of an outsider. That was the last time I was late. They pretty much scared me into being 15 minutes early for everything.

After the meeting, the entire coaching staff put us through a lengthy warm-up that involved calisthenics and several drills. During the warm-up, the coaches took turns yelling at us, "Pay attention! Focus! Push yourself! Effort! More effort! Do it right! Pay attention to detail!" Even stretching was intense.

Everyone was trying to please the coaches, but none of us were used to this. The last thing we wanted was to be singled out by a coach. It was like being in the Marines albeit in an environment of organized chaos. Head Coach Jim Marshall let the staff go wild on the incoming freshman class. I'll never forget the look on some of their faces. Some were straight-up scared. These were kids who excelled in high school and received special treatment. Six weeks earlier, we all had been studs in our communities. Six hours into our first day of college football, we were incompetent freshman or "FNGs," short for "fucking new guys."

We split up to meet with our position coaches. My linebacker coach was a man named Ken Flajole. I didn't like him. I was told he was a good coach, but he didn't acknowledge my existence. I hated that feeling.

After our position meeting, the staff tested us in the 20-yard shuttle, broad jump, vertical leap, sit-and-reach, bench press, and squat. The coaches stood over us and screamed during every test, telling us how horrible we were and how we needed work. My numbers were awful except for the bench press and squat. I went back to my dorm room that night, tired from a long day, and tried to figure out what I had gotten myself into. I came to Richmond to play for Coach Reid. He was gone but there I was at a school I didn't even know existed a year earlier. I was pissed off and irritated but I still was excited to play college football.

I was a linebacker and I often was put on the defensive line scout team during practice. Every week, our job was to replicate the other team's defense and give our starting offensive line a chance to see what they'd be going up against. Our real job was to be punching bags and take punishment. It was my first year in the program and I was going up against guys three to four years older so I was supposed to suck, but our freshman group was a little different. We looked at it as an opportunity to show the staff what we could do. We went hard as hell and tried to smack the offense in the mouth. We weren't going to be anyone's punching bag. We wanted to make practice harder than the game for the offensive line.

Every incoming freshman at Richmond expected to get redshirted. That meant we would sit out the entire season without losing a year of eligibility. It was frustrating but I didn't go in expecting to play so I was okay with it. I just wanted to get strong and adapt to university life. That first year of college was not what I hoped it would be. I tried to enjoy the process but it was difficult. The Richmond football team had a terrible season and there was negative energy surrounding the program. Just when I was starting to wonder if coming to Richmond was a mistake, something incredible happened that nobody on the team saw coming.

In the spring of my freshman year, Assistant Athletic Director Barry Barnum told me that Head Coach Jim Marshall was stepping down and they were scouting for a new coach. High on that list of candidates was Jim Reid. Richmond wanted to get Coach Reid back because of the energy he brought to the program and the way that he conducted himself. He was coming off a great year at Boston College. He helped lead that program to a winning season and a victory against Kansas State in the Aloha Bowl. It didn't take the university long to make it official and hire Jim Reid as the new head coach. I couldn't believe it. Everything worked out after all. I would get to play four

Coach Cullen worked us into the ground at practice to make game day a reward.

My big brother Mike started to feel like the little brother.

Mr. Fitz looked out for me when no one else did.

years under Coach Reid, which was what I had set out to do when I initially signed with Richmond.

Coach Reid immediately pumped new life into the program. Everything changed and the program began moving in a positive new direction. There are college football programs and then there are Jim Reid football programs. Coach Reid ran his program like a military institution. He expected everyone to be an overachiever.

It started on day one. I woke up early, attended the freshmen lifting session, and ran over to the cafeteria with my roommate, Elio, for what Coach Reid called "breakfast check." It was held every Monday through Friday. He implemented this policy because he wanted the players to know that it wasn't only about football—it was about their succeeding as men. He wanted to make sure each player started the day off with a substantial breakfast and that each player was going to class. One by one, we'd walk over to check in with either Coach Reid or an assistant.

Breakfast check was never a problem for me because I loved to eat in the cafeteria. It was beautiful and clean and you never had to worry about running out of food. The staff was made up of an exceptional group of ladies who took great care of the athletes. They snuck us food so we didn't have to wait in line. Sometimes we ate meals with them when they were on break. They quickly became like the moms we needed while living far away from home, and they were there to give us hugs when we needed them the most.

I never missed a meal but I can't say the same for some of my teammates. The consequences of missing breakfast check were simple. If you missed once, you would be punished by an early morning run at 6:00 a.m. The second offense was a much more intense run at 5:00 a.m. The third offense was a bit different. We had the great pleasure of having Colonel George Ivy on our support staff as the coordinator of academic advising for student-athletes. He served as a helicopter pilot for nearly 30 years and was awarded the Bronze Star and Purple Heart while in Vietnam. His mission at Richmond was to ensure that every student-athlete had what it took to do well athletically and also be successful in the classroom. Highly respected by the coaching staff and all the players, he and Coach Reid became close friends. Somewhere along the way, they realized that the weight of an M16 was almost the exact weight of the metal chairs used at the practice facility. The chairs became the perfect accessory for strike three, and Coach Reid would make the offender run quarter-mile repeats with the chair over his head.

If you continually missed breakfast, the staff not only made your life a living hell but the team would be subjected to extra conditioning while you sat in a chair and watched. Those types of problems were usually fixed quickly because the team took matters into their own hands. Coach Reid preached responsibility and accountability, saying, "We are only as strong as our weakest link. We all have a responsibility to each other."

After breakfast, we rolled out of the dining hall and headed to our first class. A literature class called Core, it was a favorite at Richmond. We were required to read 15 books over the course of the semester. We'd discuss them in class and be tested on the material. The coaching staff liked it because it forced students to think and talk openly in a classroom setting. I liked the course, but it was the first time I was asked to share my views with classmates. A part of me was nervous, but I enjoyed the way it challenged me to think about life.

The first book was *White Noise* by Don DeLillo. I had read the book so when the professor asked for someone to discuss the plot, I raised my hand.

"The book is about a young man's struggle with life and living with the decisions he made that hindered his success," I said. I was pleased with my response but the professor wasn't impressed.

"That's not what it's about at all," he replied. "Did you even read the book?"

"Yes, sir."

The truth was that I read the book twice but I didn't understand what I was reading and had trouble retaining information. Still, I felt like my answer was solid and that the teacher only called me out because I was an athlete. He resented that I was given a first-class education that I didn't necessarily deserve. I knew that there were times when I was out of my league academically, but I felt like I belonged there. I had been through a lot of shit for the right to sit in that classroom. No one was going to tell me I didn't belong. I didn't care what the professor thought. I would continue to add my two cents and make the most out of my time in class.

Speech class with Dr. David Thomas was one of my favorites. He was a big man who wore glasses and took teaching to heart. He played football back in the day and looked like he would've been a great lineman because of his size. The point of the course was learning how to speak to a group in an organized manner and he made sure we all contributed. That was a big fear of mine, but Dr. Thomas built us up just like a coach. He was calm and focused. He explained in great detail how to approach a speech. He was the first professor who took his time with us and made sure we were ready to hit the stage with great confidence. We started out with a short speech, only a few minutes long, and worked all the way up to speaking for 30 to 40 minutes. I didn't know it at the time but that would prepare me for some great speeches in the future.

Just because I liked class didn't mean that I was doing well. Football alone was a huge responsibility. The added academic pressure became a burden that I couldn't handle. The average student had three to four classes each day. The football players were taking a standard course load, plus a two-hour lift session, three-hour practice, and a one-hour film session. I was overwhelmed and I quickly fell behind. My high school teachers understood how I best retained information and went to great lengths to help me succeed. College was a different ball game. I didn't miss a single class and I still had an awful 1.6 GPA.

Coach Reid saw that several of the freshmen were struggling and immediately implemented mandatory study hall. That meant that any free moment outside of the classroom, football, and training was spent in the Robins Center catching up on school work. Your year didn't matter. If you had a GPA below 3.0, you were forced to attend study hall. Some nights, it was held after practice; other times, it was held during the day and even on weekends. Coach Reid constantly checked up on us. Study hall helped me, but I needed more. I needed someone to guide me through my homework and break things down so I could understand.

The man in charge of study hall was a local high school teacher named Mr. Barry Gibbral. He always had a big smile on his face and a well-groomed, salt-and-pepper beard that he stroked whenever he was thinking. At the start of my second semester, Coach Reid personally introduced us.

"Mr. Gibbral, this is Marc Megna. Marc is struggling with his Core class and needs help with his writing."

Mr. Gibbral gave me a firm handshake. "It's a pleasure to meet you, Marc. Pull up a chair. Let's see how we can help you along."

That was the start of a great friendship. Each night, Mr. Gibbral would arrive at study hall with a giant pile of books under his arm and a stack of papers to grade, but he always took the time to help me better understand the books I read for my Core class. I'd hand him the book and he'd tell me to come back in 15 minutes. It turned out that Mr. Gibbral was a speed reader who could get through an entire book in record time. It amazed me how he could retain so much information.

Mr. Gibbral guided me through each book and encouraged me. I used to toil away on my computer, trying to write papers for class, and wind up getting a C. I didn't understand what I was doing wrong and I was embarrassed that my work was below average, but Mr. Gibbral always reminded me of the progress I had made. He pointed out the things I did well. I wouldn't have been able to cut it academically at Richmond without him.

When I struggled in the classroom back in high school, I always found solace playing football but things weren't going according to plan on the field either. I learned at the beginning of the year that Coach Reid wanted to move me from linebacker to defensive line. He penciled me in as starting nose guard, which came as a shock to me since I had never played the position before. I was only 219 pounds and would be lining up against guys who were over 300 pounds. I was going to get my ass handed to me. I told him, "Coach, I don't know if I'm big enough."

"You can do it. You will do it. You'll be great," he said. "Now get out of my office."

I may have been a linebacker in high school but I didn't know how to play linebacker. I wasn't fundamentally sound. I was just a kid who played like a maniac and did everything full speed. Coach Reid knew that I was going to be a defensive lineman the whole time. He thought I had decent speed but he always questioned my ability to change direction. He liked the idea of my chasing down the quarterback as an edge player.

Coach Reid wanted to have all of his most athletic, energetic, and highly productive athletes on the field at the same time. He didn't give a shit what position I played. We had one guy who wasn't a particularly good safety so Coach Reid moved him to linebacker. Now we had a kid who ran like a deer playing outside linebacker. All of the defensive linemen were former linebackers who were moved to the line. When piecing together the new program at Richmond, he kept stressing the same thing—play fast and don't worry about making mistakes. He didn't care if we jumped off sides. He wanted us to come off the ball fast and not to let up or play cautiously.

"Key the ball. Get a great first step, and fly off the snap," he told us.

I'll never forget Coach Reid's words to me as a freshman: "No matter what, just keep coming, Marc!"

Not only was I about to learn a brand-new position, but I was about to cross paths with the most insane wild man I've ever played for—Joe Cullen, the defensive line coach. I could probably write an entire book about him because the man was a straight-up lunatic. Coach Reid recruited Coach Cullen, a Quincy native, as a non-scholarship player back when he coached the University of Massachusetts. He may have been an undersized defensive lineman but he started every game of his four-year career. He spent a year as a graduate assistant and then became a position coach before making the transition with Coach Reid to the University of Richmond. I didn't know it at the time but Coach Reid and Coach Cullen would be responsible for getting me to the NFL.

Being a defensive lineman under Joe Cullen meant a few things. First, it meant that you would get coached extremely hard, harder than anything you could imagine. You'd be pushed right to the edge and to a point where it felt like you couldn't take any more. Second, it meant you'd be doing more drills, reps, and running than any other field position. Not everyone could take that style of coaching. Coach Cullen struck fear in the hearts of most guys on the team. Some guys would claim that his antics didn't faze them, but most guys melted when he got in their face and dropped the hammer.

In college, Coach Cullen played the game going 100 miles per hour all the time. That carried over into his coaching style. He believed that playing with great energy could take the life right out of our opponent and that if we outworked and were more intense than our opponent, we would win.

We've all had coaches who've yelled but Coach Cullen was different. His yell was more of a violent roar. Most people didn't know what to make of this crazy, intense coach who constantly screamed. They'd wonder if it was all for show because nobody could possibly keep up that intense pace. Well, he did. He was just as intense during the last hour of the last practice as he was during the first.

When I was a freshman, a redshirt defensive end named Lee Owens was so intimidated that he would vomit every time Coach Cullen yelled at him. It was unbelievable. It didn't matter what he was doing. If we were stretching and Coach raised his voice, Lee would throw up whatever he ate for lunch. It happened every practice without fail. I felt terrible for the poor kid and remember thinking that Coach Cullen would never get away with that stuff in the NFL. He'd probably get his ass kicked by some player who didn't want to take his shit, but I was wrong. He went on to coach defensive line for multiple NFL teams, including Detroit, Jacksonville, Cleveland, Tampa, and Baltimore. Nothing changed. I've heard stories about him getting into screaming matches with some of the best players in the league and throwing some of his NFL players out of meeting rooms. It didn't matter to him if he was coaching at the collegiate or the NFL level, he coached the exact same way.

He made us practice at a crazy high tempo so we would play at a crazy high tempo. He wanted us soaked to the bone in sweat, regardless of the day of the week. He didn't care if it was only the walk-through practice the day before the game. One day, he asked me, "Do you know why Mike Tyson is the best fighter of his time?"

"Because he's tougher?"

"It's because he spars the same way he fights."

That's the approach that Joe Cullen took to coaching.

Practice became a new level of torture. I couldn't believe how fucking hard it was and that was only after the first one. I was dragging through the first session and knew that we had another one in the afternoon. I didn't think that there was a man alive who could maintain that tempo. I found out later that Coach was weeding out guys who were lazy and didn't play with heart or passion because their negative energy would be a cancer that spread through the rest of the team. Hardworking overachievers who would do whatever it took were the only ones welcomed into his defensive line unit.

He was trying to beat us down and it was working. But between practice and school, it all became too much. I started to think that I didn't have what they expected. I called my mom back in Fall River. I told her what was going on and that I was thinking of coming home, which meant that I'd lose my scholarship.

She said, "Marc, if you give up now, I won't say anything, but you will kick yourself in the ass every day for the rest of your life."

My mother was always there when I needed her, and she knew how to put the situation into perspective.

"Sometimes in life, you don't have to do extraordinary things," she said. "You just have to hang in there."

She knew that I didn't sound good. A couple of days later, she FedExed me a package along with a letter. She attached a Post-it Note that read: "Dream Big & Never Quit." I read that note, and I cried. I knew that I could be the first person in our family to graduate from college and how much that meant to her. I couldn't let her down.

I put that note above my bed so it was the first thing I'd see in the morning and the last thing I'd see at night. That little piece of paper triggered something inside of me. From that day forward, I approached everything with a different attitude both on the field and in the classroom. I was going to bust my ass. If I did that, then I didn't have to worry about the outcome. If I failed, that was fine, but I was going to give everything I had during every practice and in every class. I remembered what got me to that point. I needed to get that confidence back, and it changed how I would do things for the rest of my life. Even today, if I'm going to sign my name to something, I make sure that I give it everything I have.

At practice, when we'd break from stretching, I started sprinting to defensive line drills so I'd be first. There I was, a freshman, and I was the one setting the tempo. My teammates thought I was nuts. It pissed off some of the upperclassmen.

Jason Giska grabbed me and said, "Freshman in the back!"

I said, "Fuck you! If you want to get to the front, you're gonna have to beat me here every single day."

We went at it, but I refused to give up my spot.

The next day, he said, "If you beat me, you deserve to be here!"

Every day, I got to the front of that line. I didn't want to make anyone look bad, but I couldn't allow myself to be lazy. I wanted my attitude to rub off on them in a positive way. Soon, even Coach Cullen took notice. I still had no idea what I was doing, but he would point out my performance during a film session and say, "This is the effort we need to win a championship."

Coach Cullen and Coach Reid recruited particular players. They looked for guys with relentless motors. Not a guy who screams and yells but a guy who gives his best effort. Effort is not hard to spot. Coaches can push players, but they can't get maximum effort out of their players unless the athlete demands it from himself. He must commit and put out. He must be a fierce competitor who refuses to give up. He must be an enforcer who doesn't shy away from contact or back down. He must lead by example and practice his ass off. He must be able to call out a teammate when necessary and stand up for others when they can't stand up for themselves. Those are the real leaders. The coaching staff may have the pulse of the team but it's the players who decide on the leaders. We were fortunate enough at Richmond to have several highly motivated overachievers because those are the guys who cause lots of problems for the opponent.

The coaches also made sure that we were conditioned. They forced the defense to perform in a chaotic environment. When scrimmaging, they'd have one offensive unit set up and run a play against the defense and then send in a second offensive unit to run another play without a rest. The offense would keep rotating, but the defense would remain on the field. At first, we were all sucking wind, but we got used to it pretty quick.

As Coach Reid said, "Men, we must be the best-conditioned team in America! No one will be in better condition than us."

I'd love to meet a team that was in better shape. It felt like I was at one of the military academies. The coaches made us do everything with a sense of urgency. Our goal was to be first at everything. The philosophy of the program was to give it your all. The guys who bought into that concept grew within the program and had positive collegiate careers while those who fought the system never fulfilled the expectations of the staff.

It took a long time but I learned to appreciate the way Coach Cullen pushed me. When a coach is hard on you, it means that they care. When they ignore you and don't say anything, then you have a problem. That guy wanted me to be better and I knew he would make me as good as I could be.

The season was a grind. Every week was the same. Our rivals didn't matter. Coach Cullen made them all seem like All-Pros. It started off with a defensive unit meeting. He went over our opponent's strengths while showing us a tape of their previous game and season highlights. He told us what to look out for and how we'd get our ass kicked if we weren't prepared. And he did it all while drenched in sweat and screaming in his hoarse voice. He would never give us any credit before the game. He had high expectations for us all and it didn't matter if you were a freshman or a senior. Upperclassmen knew the drill. Underclassman had heard all the stories but they were still in for a rude awakening.

After the unit meeting, we broke off to go to our position meetings. Those were epic. It always felt like Coach Cullen was going to rip the door off the hinges when he barged into the classroom. He was already amped up from the previous meeting and picked back up right where he left off.

"Sit up straight," he said. "Put your feet on the floor and don't take your eyes off me!"

We had to keep our heads up, our eyes open, and have a pen in our hands. You were not allowed to yawn under any circumstances. If you got caught, he either kicked you out or forced you to stand on your chair for the duration of the meeting.

If there was one thing you would learn while under his tutelage, it was detail. "Pay attention to detail and you will learn it," he said over and over again.

I always had trouble retaining information in school but our coaching staff at Richmond found a way to teach us every play in the 300-page playbook. Coach would draw the play on the board and repeat the information. He would then call on each of us to step up to the board and teach it the others. At any given time, I could be called to the grease board to review the entire defense. I had to know each player's alignment and responsibility. Coach Cullen was in my ear the whole time.

"Where does the three-technique line up?" he asked. "What's his job if the guard pulls? Where does the nose line up? What's his job? Quick! What's the strong side end's responsibility?"

By the end of the meeting, we had it all down cold. The whole time, he'd pump us up, saying, "We better fly around the field and set the tempo! Energy! Energy! Energy! No one will outwork us!"

Coach Cullen knew exactly how to push my buttons and could manipulate my emotions like no other coach. He had ties to UMass so before our game against them, he told us what he heard they had said about me.

"Megna who? That's what they said," he told me. "We're gonna kick Megna's ass! He's too small. Let's run right at him."

Back then, I was far from being level-headed so I took that as the ultimate sign of disrespect. I knew he was trying to hype me up but it still bothered me. UMass was the school that told me I wasn't good enough so I wanted to make sure they would regret their decision.

Once we broke up the meeting, the defensive linemen had about 15 minutes to be in pads and out on the field to cover the day's installation before everyone else. All the defensive linemen were instructed to tape their hands, fingers, and thumbs like boxers. Each finger was taped above and below each joint to avoid jamming. When properly taped, it felt like you had metal rods for fingers.

I sprained my thumbs several times a year. They got so bad that head trainer Chris Hanks molded two plastic casts for my thumbs. They fit perfectly, and I could punch the steel facemasks of an offensive lineman and not worry about injury.

We started practice by stretching with the captains in the middle and then sprinted full speed to position drills. Coach Cullen wanted practice to be hell so the games would feel like slow motion. The defensive line was the heartbeat of the entire team, and it was understood that we would set the tempo. If you weren't aggressive and fast, you had to do it again. Hell, even if you were fast, Coach Cullen would yell, "Do it again!"

I would line back up and start the drill over. Coach snapped the ball. I'd smack the center in the mouth and put him on his ass but it was still not good enough.

"Do it again!" Coach Cullen yelled.

I started to get pissed, but I'd do it again.

"Nope! Not good enough, Marc! You're going to have to come off the ball harder than that!"

I lined back up and started over.

"Do it again! Do it again! Do it again!"

It was like that with every drill during every practice, and we typically did a drill up to 10 times before we were let off the hook. He wanted to squeeze the last bit of effort out of every player. That sent a message to the entire defensive unit that the best players were coached the hardest.

A coach can be hard on his players, but a coach should never degrade his players. There's a big difference between "Get your fucking ass to the ball!" and "You're a fucking ass!" The latter is just poor coaching.

Coach Cullen always told his players not to mistake yelling for anger. That was just the way he coached. The only way he knew how to do it was with passion. He also knew how to read his players, and he didn't treat them all the same. He could tell who could endure tough coaching and who couldn't. I'm not sure what tipped him off but he immediately recognized he could coach me hard. He would push me to the brink, but just when I reached my lowest point and was about to break, he would pull me back up. What was good about Coach Cullen was that he'd always let you know when you made a great play. And he let you know in front of your peers. He may have been hard but players grew to respect him because they knew he had their backs and would go through a brick wall for them. When a player knows that he's going to be rewarded for something great, it makes him want to push harder. And he knew how to keep his players hungry. If you had four sacks in a game, Coach Cullen's job was to knock you off your pedestal and make you want to do better.

During one practice my sophomore year before a Delaware game, Coach Cullen kept me on the field for an extra hour to work on the "Influence Trap." I had screwed it up the entire practice, and he didn't feel right about ending practice on a low note. After he sent everyone in, I stayed on the field for another hour. I hit the blocking board and simulated the proper steps. When the team trainer, Chris Hanks, tried to get me off the field, I slammed my helmet on the ground and threw my shoulder pads into the woods.

Pieces of my equipment went flying everywhere. I was tired, irritated, and emotional.

Hanks told me, "Pick your shit up and grow up."

"I'm staying out here," I said. "I'm not going in yet."

I stayed on the field after practice that day and hit the buck-board more than 100 times. Hanks was a great guy whom everyone liked very much but on that day, he was in a panic when he got back to the locker room.

"We got a problem, Coach Cullen. Megs is still on the field. He threw his pads and helmet."

"Good," Coach Cullen responded. "He needs the work. Leave him there. He'll be fine."

To Hanks, it looked like a mental breakdown and honestly, it kind of was. But to Coach Cullen, it was par for the course and it meant that he had me in the mental state necessary for optimal performance.

That week I had my best game of the year. It was proof that his type of coaching worked well for me. As much as I hate to admit it, I responded very well to his antics and thrived in that harsh environment.

When I became an upperclassman, practices didn't get any easier. In fact, they got much harder, but I was ready. The secret was that I took it one play at a time. Regardless of what the coaching staff threw at us, I always came back with a smile and loved every single minute of it. I was no longer just trying to survive—I was there to take charge.

When we were running sprints and everyone was dog-tired, I would pump my legs, run hard, breathe deep, give everything I had, and sell the fuck out on that one sprint. It didn't matter if we had to run ten more. Fuck it! If I couldn't do the next one, so be it, but I could do that one. I was still exhausted, but I trained myself to do that every single play and it became the standard I set for myself. That energy was contagious and could pick up the entire team. Later, people would ask me how I could keep going, and I told them, "I never saved anything for the next play." That's how I approached the rest of my football career and it made all the difference.

My production on the field was the byproduct of my conditioning and the constant drilling I received during practice. Repetition is the mother of learning, and when you do the same thing correctly, it becomes a habit. I saw the plays in practice so many times that I began to react faster than ever, without thinking. I hated Coach Cullen while he was kicking my ass during practice but on game day, I was always grateful he was hard on me.

Making the move to defensive line meant that I had to gain weight, which was no easy task. Because we did so much conditioning, I dropped to under 220 during my redshirt year. I was like a skeleton because we were running so much. I couldn't keep weight on for the life of me. I was able to get back up to 225 for my freshman season, but as a 225-pound nose guard, I was getting my ass kicked. Coach Reid kept playing me.

Once I got my technique down and learned how to manipulate the offensive lineman, I started to make a bunch of crazy plays. I may have looked like a linebacker, but I was strong enough to muscle people around at the line and also fast enough to run people down in the backfield.

Still, 225 wasn't going to cut it. I needed to get bigger so I could anchor down for double-teams and withstand the pounding I took in the trenches. That meant I had to eat. Lots of guys on the team were light eaters and would stick to the traditional bowl of sugary cereal, but I went all out. Breakfast usually consisted of one large Belgium waffle with peanut butter, eight egg whites, two toasted bagels, one large bowl of oatmeal, and an entire omelet for good measure. Now and then I would add an extra waffle.

The metabolism of a young person is usually through the roof. The constant weight training, running, and practice revved it up even more. I was able to get up to 240 pounds my sophomore year, 245 my junior year, and eventually 255 my senior year. And I did it without losing any speed. When you play for Jim Reid and Joe Cullen, you're basically on a track team. Lineman shouldn't be doing 400-yard and 800-yard sprints around the track. But we were and our endurance was off the charts. Sometimes during two-a-days, we'd go through a hundred snaps in addition to practice drills. I could have eaten a large pizza every night and still lost seven pounds a day. It was so hard to keep weight on.

None of that meant anything if I didn't perform on the field and make plays. I was getting better but a noticeable shift occurred during the last game of my sophomore year against the College of William & Mary. We were having a terrible year with a 2-9 record and things only got worse in that last game. The team played awful. The game was out of reach, but I was still playing hard and personally, I had a great game. I had nine tackles and two sacks but it was all in a losing effort. That year I ended up making the All-Conference team as a sophomore, in spite of our record, which gave me a tremendous amount of confidence that carried over into my junior year. I realized that if I just played every game as I did against William & Mary, my numbers would be better than everyone—not only on our team or in our conference but in the entire country.

That's exactly what I did and my junior year felt like a coming out party. The team did so much better. Every game I had one or two sacks and two or three tackles for a loss. By the end of the year, I had more than 100 tackles, 35 tackles for a loss, and 13 sacks. People started to notice.

In the summer before my senior year, while everyone else went back home and partied, I stayed on campus at Richmond. Some of my teammates would come and go but I was there the entire time, often by myself just training hard. I never took time off.

I'd be out there in the middle of the field in the scalding heat working on my technique. Anyone watching me from across the street must have thought I was a lunatic. Picture a kid in the middle of the summer going through his steps on the field. It looked like I was dancing out there and I did hundreds and hundreds of reps. Nobody wanted to do that kind of technique work. Guys say they want to play at the next level but very few want to put in the amount of work needed to get there. All of those reps, and that little bit extra, are what helped me.

Meanwhile, I waited for the release of the *College Football Preview* magazine. Every couple of days, I'd go over to Barnes & Noble to see when it would arrive. I must have made four or five trips and asked everyone in the store, but one day I saw it sitting there on the shelf. I was nervous. I knew the 1-AA section, where they listed the top players in the country at each position, was in the back of the magazine. The first thing I saw was the list for defensive lineman and there was my name. I was listed as the number one defensive lineman in the country.

Growing up, I was the kid the coaches only put in the game because they felt bad for me. I was an average linebacker in high school. Then I got to college and was moved to a position that I was too small for. There were constant obstacles and setbacks. Finally, it felt like I was starting to get recognized. When I was a kid, I told myself that I was going to be in that magazine and there I was, looking at my name in print. Right there in the middle of Barnes & Noble, I broke down crying. A middle-aged woman next to me reading *Better Homes and Gardens* looked over and I told her, "I'm sorry, I'm just really happy."

I still have that magazine today, and I keep it in my office for motivation.

I still have this sticky note from my moms letter.
It still motivates me today.

WHAT I LEARNED

Whatever you think your limits, you can break through them. Push until the very end, and you will be surprised at what you are capable of achieving. Don't ever assume that it's over or that things have to be a certain way. The second you become content is the second you compromise your outcome.

CHAPTER 7

GETTING READY FOR THE NFL

"[If] a thing is humanly possible, consider it to be within your reach."

—Roman Emperor Marcus Aurelius

The 1998 Richmond football team finished 9-2, the best record in school history. We were eliminated in the first round of the 1-AA playoffs, but I was happy that we finally turned the program around. The staff and my teammates were people whom I was able to depend on for anything. The bond we formed was priceless and being a part of that special group of brothers was a privilege. I'm still very close to my former teammates. Whenever we talk today, I can feel the strong connection that we built as a team. It's one thing to have a friend. It's completely different to have a group of reliable people you can call for help when you hit a rough patch.

I was sad that my time at Richmond was coming to an end but there was still a lot that I needed to accomplish. It was time for the final push before I could fulfill my lifelong dream of playing in the National Football League.

I was fortunate enough to be selected to play in the Hooters Hula Bowl. Bob Thalman, a longtime coach for Virginia Military Institute, pushed to get me on the roster and it was a huge honor to be selected. The Hula Bowl was just one of the many college all-star games that provided seniors an opportunity to play alongside and against the best players in the country.

There were other games, including the Senior Bowl, East West Shrine, and Gridiron Classic, but it's safe to say that the Hula Bowl in Honolulu was definitely the most relaxed. I was excited to get my first up-close look at the rest of the NFL hopefuls in our draft class.

Before traveling to Hawaii, all the players were flown to San Francisco where we went through several physical and mental tests, including the infamous Wonderlic group intelligence test with 50 questions that must be answered in 12 minutes. The questions are not especially difficult but the compressed time frame can make them seem more challenging. Although the Wonderlic has been used in many occupations, it is most famous as being the aptitude—or IQ—test for NFL prospects. I had heard stories about the Wonderlic test and its difficulty, so I was nervous.

One of our coaches said, "After you take the test, you fall into one of two categories. Some guys will play for an NFL team and others will own an NFL team."

They put all the players in a classroom-like setting, handed out the test, and set the clock for 12 minutes. The questions started off easy and then became more difficult. What's interesting about the test is that you never learn your score unless you're the smartest or dumbest guy in the group. I never heard my score so I assumed that I was neither.

Later that day, we flew to Hawaii and settled into our hotel rooms. We stayed at the same hotel that hosted the players for the NFL Pro Bowl. At first, I was assigned to play for the South but was later placed on the North team because of an imbalance in roster numbers. Our head coach was Lloyd Carr from the University of Michigan. He had a great reputation as a winning coach and was well liked by all the coaches. We also had several assistant coaches who had won their conferences and were great teachers of the game.

The two teams were comprised primarily of players from the big power conferences like the SEC and Big Ten. I stood at 6'2" and 250 pounds and felt like a shrimp next to the rest of those guys. Most of the players were really friendly. There were a few guys who were too cool to hang with the rest of the group but for the most part it was a positive environment. Everyone was focused on the task at hand and wanted to make a positive first impression on the coaches and scouts who would be watching us that week.

We had to attend a series of events and had some great guides to escort us around and give us the lay of the land. They went over the rules and the dress code for the week: T-shirts and shorts only, no button-down shirts or ties allowed. Playing in the Hula Bowl was reward enough for a great collegiate career but we also received lots of free gifts that week. Every time we went to an event, we came back with a bag filled with T-shirts, shorts, and sweat suits.

The dinner that first evening was held in a large banquet hall packed with tables and a giant buffet equipped to handle the massive appetites of two football teams. Once we were all seated, they opened the doors to the banquet hall and in walked 50 girls dressed in skirts and heels. Each girl had won the bikini contest in her respective state and was now vying for the title of Miss Hooters USA.

After dinner, the team and some of the girls went to the Jacuzzi for drinks. It was an entertaining evening but I couldn't completely enjoy myself. I thought everything was some kind of character test so I became paranoid. I'm still not convinced that it wasn't. I just wanted to focus on practice and the upcoming game. Not hanging out and taking part in the social activities was difficult but I looked at it as a personal victory. If you can watch dozens of girls in thongs make their way down to the pool for a party and still opt to return to your room to spend the night alone, you know your head is on straight. From my hotel room, I could hear all the shenanigans happening down at the pool but I somehow managed to fall asleep.

We practiced that week at a local high school before NFL coaches and scouts. I felt like I was under a microscope. Players were being evaluated on hustle, team play, and how they processed information. I made sure to run everywhere I went. It didn't matter if we had a water break, I ran there.

Coaches kept the defensive plays simple so players could be graded on their natural ability. Sometimes we had to switch things up on the fly, and when that happened, everyone wanted to be the guy who could understand the modification and then flawlessly implement it. If we were running a defensive stunt and it was my job to clear a path for the blitzing linebacker, I wanted to make sure he had a runway so he could look like a star. It wasn't just me. Everyone had that mentality. Since these were the best players in the country, there was no shortage of confidence.

The wide receivers and defensive backs would get mouthy when running drills together. The defensive backs always talked lots of shit. The one-on-ones between the offensive and defensive linemen were much different. The nature of those positions didn't allow for much talking. They did the grunt work so they did most of their communicating through cold stares.

That drill still got pretty intense. I no longer rushed against the smaller 1-AA linemen. I now faced guys like Josh Heskew of Nebraska, Jon Jansen of Michigan, and Brian Connolly of Army. They were huge. Jansen stood 6'6" and weighed 310 pounds. He looked like a bulked-up NBA forward. I often gave away 60 and sometimes 80 pounds. A smaller guy like me had to use my speed to get to the edge of the offensive lineman. That was the first rule of pass rushing. Get the lineman to move his feet and then beat him on the corner or get him to change his direction as quickly as possible. When the guy in front of me expected speed, I would take it right down the middle for a good old-fashioned bull rush. I won a few and lost a few. I had a nice up-and-under move but got buried a few times as well. Either way, I always bounced back up and finished the drill. Whenever I got rolled or driven in the ground, I certainly felt it.

On the night of the traditional family-style Hawaiian Luau dinner, Coach Carr reminded us to stay focused. He knew the bikini contest girls would be roaming the hotel so he warned us not to get any silicone in our mouths, saying, "It's poisonous and you could get sick." It was refreshing to hear someone who took the game so seriously crack a few jokes.

That night, we got to eat like kings and spend time with our teammates. I even bumped into a fellow player from Massachusetts named Sean Morey. That name sounded familiar. It took me a little while to place him but as we talked, I remembered him as the speedy receiver from Marshfield High against whom I competed at Durfee. He was about 5'11" tall, 185 pounds, and in ridiculous shape. Sean had a reputation as a workhorse who could run, but he was humble and a class act. He also was smart as a whip, having just graduated from Brown. He set the Ivy League record with 251 receptions, 3,850 total yards, and 40 touchdowns. He finished his career second in all-time receiving yards in Division I-AA behind only Jerry Rice. That's not bad at all.

I also spent time with Jerry Azumah from the University of New Hampshire. I had played against Jerry while at Richmond. Another Massachusetts native, he set the Division I-AA career rushing record with 6,193 yards. He also set the Division I-AA record with 8,276 career all-purpose yards. He was an amazing athlete who was incredibly shifty and played like he was possessed. We had respect for each other but never passed up an opportunity to bust balls so I had to keep reminding him how easily Richmond handled UNH.

It was great being surrounded by a few 1-AA guys. Both Sean and Jerry were perfect examples of how it didn't matter how big you were or where you played. If you were a talented and productive player, you would be given an opportunity. We had earned the right to be there and to play with the nation's best.

One night at the hotel, I walked into the team room as a muscled-up guy with dreadlocks walked in. He was soft spoken and tried not to draw attention to himself. It was Heisman Trophy winner Ricky Williams. The media made him out to be arrogant and tough but he was friendly, polite, and very shy. He was just an ordinary guy. I learned that night not to believe everything I heard. Yes, he was 5'11" and 230 pounds and looked like he was carved out of a block of granite but he was very humble. We were all under pressure to perform well but I could tell that the pressure on him was even greater.

Being a Heisman Trophy winner comes with tremendous expectations. We were all aware of the "Heisman curse" that sometimes affected players when they reached the NFL and resulted in sub-par careers but Ricky appeared to be different. He ran wild in college and most scouts felt that he would make a smooth transition and become a productive NFL player. I had the same feeling. That night, all we did was talk and play video games but I walked away from that experience as a huge Ricky Williams fan.

The actual Hula Bowl game was anticlimactic. I was excited to play but the scouts were there to watch the week of practice. Many didn't even stick around for the game. It was difficult to be productive in an all-star game like that because players either played the first and third quarters or the second and fourth quarters. You weren't out there long enough to get anything done. One great play could get you Defensive MVP honors.

After the Hula Bowl, the next step was the NFL Scouting Combine. The combine was a week-long showcase held every February at the RCA Dome (now Lucas Oil Stadium) in Indianapolis. It was invitation only, and the top draft-eligible college football players in the country would perform a series of physical and mental tests in front of NFL coaches, general managers, and scouts. Performance at the combine could impact draft status, salary, and ultimately a player's career so when I found out that I wasn't on the invite list, I was pissed. The majority of the players were from big 1A schools. There were a few 1-AA players invited but for whatever reason, I didn't make the cut. I looked at it as just another obstacle that I needed to overcome in order to earn the respect of the scouts.

I wouldn't be attending the combine but I would still get the chance to test in front of scouts in mid-March. Lots of the top players had agents front the cash for them to attend a performance center that specialized in prepping college players for the draft. My agent, Jack Mula, was very good. He looked out for me but I felt that I'd be okay on my own. Looking back, it definitely would have helped to learn the ins and outs from a performance guru.

In the spring, I had enough credits to graduate from college. I wasn't allowed to stay in the dorms but since I was working as a graduate assistant coach in the football program, they found a room for me in a converted storage closet in the athletic facility. That's where I lived while getting ready for the draft.

What's funny was that I once again was categorized as a linebacker because of my size. I was a linebacker in high school only to arrive at Richmond, where I was told I wasn't good enough and moved to defensive line. Now I was too small to be a lineman, and they were talking about me becoming a linebacker again. So be it. No matter what position they wanted me to play, I was going to be ready.

Darin Thomas, Richmond's strength coach, offered his services to help me get ready for the big day. He was a hardworking coach who helped players any way he could. Each day, he took me, safety Winston October, and running back Jasper Pendergrass out to the turf field and ran us through the six drills we'd be tested on during our pro day: The 40-yard dash, vertical jump, broad jump, 3-cone drill, shuttle run, and bench press. All we had was a handheld video camera and a tape measure. We'd perform up to 30 reps of each drill. After we finished, we'd spend hours watching the tape so we could critique each rep. Reps, Reps, Reps! I did so many reps that I could do those drills in my sleep.

The bench test involved pressing 225 pounds for as many reps as possible. I had tested my one-rep max at Richmond and was able to press 435 pounds, but preparing for this test was tricky because pressing 225 for reps required using an entirely different endurance level to attract scouts. Anybody could have a high one-rep max but being able to do a lot of reps at 225 told scouts how often you frequented the college weight room. I had to make sure to prepare my body for what to expect but not strain or tear a muscle by overtraining.

The shuttle run and the 3-cone drill tested lateral quickness and explosion in short spaces. Those drills were about busting your ass and pushing yourself to get the best time possible. The 40-yard dash was the marquee event at the combine. It was like the 100-meter dash at the Olympics. That one was all about explosion and speed. The vertical jump and the broad jump were used to measure lower-body explosion and power. I was conditioned so the running drills didn't worry me much. Still, we worked those drills for a couple months so I improved and brought my times down considerably. Shawn Barber, my former teammate and good friend at Richmond, was an All-American who had been drafted the previous year. He had attended the combine so he could tell us how to approach each drill and give us some inside tips.

When my pro day arrived, I was ready. I didn't care that there were only a handful of scouts in attendance. It was nerve-wracking, but having my teammates there going through the testing with me was a huge help. We started off in the weight room for the bench press. I was shooting for 30 reps. I wanted to show them how I made the most of my weight room training. After warming up my shoulders with a few light sets, I was amped up and ready for the real thing. I lifted the bar off the rack and began to press at a brisk tempo. I hit 20 before fatigue set in. I rested for a moment with my arms locked out and then began to press in clusters of three before resting again. I hit 29. I took one brief rest at the top, and then did one more rep, then another, and another. I made it all the way to 35. They took two reps away because I didn't lock out my arms all the way, but 33 was a strong number and I was proud.

The bench was, without a doubt, the easiest part of my testing. Up next was the most challenging test—the 40-yard dash. Lots of athletes think they have speed but they don't have NFL speed. The 40 measures each draftee's straight-line athleticism. Fractions of a second can decide whether an athlete will be drafted or fall to free agency status. Before my test, I did my warm-ups in a jogging suit. I wanted to break a mild sweat. I walked over to the starting line and went over the steps in my head. I physically practiced that test hundreds of times. I firmly believed that I had to excel in my mind before I could perform physically. I had prepped for that moment my whole life. I wasn't going to screw it up.

When the gun fired, I ran like my life depended on it. I crossed the line feeling confident but a little unsure. They give you two attempts and a third, if necessary. The irritating part is they don't tell you your first time before your second run. Then again, that was probably for the best. I didn't need my mind in overdrive while I ran. I was praying that I got under 4.7 and I did. My first time was a 4.68 and my second 4.64. By no means was that blazing speed, but it was solid for an NFL linebacker.

Next were the pro agility drills. I had practiced every single day so I was confident with my technique. I ran a 4.2 in the shuttle and 7.2 in the 3-cone. Both solid. The vertical jump surprised me. I scored a 32½. I had a strong squat and power clean, which both played a huge factor in my ability to generate force. So far, I was compiling some strong numbers for a small-school defensive lineman.

The combine provides scouts with a great look at your raw athletic ability, but it isn't the be-all and end-all and it doesn't guarantee that you are a great football player. Many top prospects have put up impressive numbers at the combine but never cut it in the NFL because they couldn't transfer that strength and speed to the field. What's important is productivity. Above everything else, you have to be a good football player with a high football IQ. A 4.5 is really a 4.9 if you don't know where you're going; on this scale, a lower number is a better one. A player who lacks the capacity to process information is just another average player, which is why NFL scouts try to leave no stone unturned.

After the tests, one of the scouts put me through several linebacker-type drills to see if I could move in space. They watched my hips to see if I was stiff and how efficiently I could change direction. Since it was just me and there was nobody else taking any reps, rest was minimal. When I finished, it felt like I had gone through an entire practice. My legs were Jell-O. I met with each scout individually. They asked questions about playing in college and certain moments they had picked out from my college game films.

One of them actually asked me, "Do you think you can play in the NFL?"

"There's no question in my mind," I said.

And there wasn't. I couldn't believe someone would ask that. The way I saw it, I had played with and against guys who were making a living in the NFL. I knew I had done well by comparison.

After my pro day, I took a few days to rest. I had been tearing my body down for weeks since the season ended but I couldn't relax completely. Every few days, a scout would walk in and ask me to do all the testing again. I ended up testing out a few more times until Coach Reid put a stop to it. The beauty of the combine was that you did all the drills once and you were done. I was in a different situation because every time a scout showed up at the school, I basically had to go through another combine. It wears you down and your numbers suffer because you're not fresh. The 225-pound bench press is something you should do once a month but I was doing it a couple times a week. If I got 34 reps one day and then 26 the next day, it looked like I wasn't as strong but in reality, I was exhausted.

One of the scouts walked in on a Friday, weeks after testing, and asked me to do the bench press again. Coach Reid yelled at him and said, "Marc has done it three times this week. He'll end up tearing a pec!" Thank God for Coach Reid. He was always looking out for me. I was supposed to tell them to get the numbers off the other scouts who had been at my pro day but the last thing I wanted to do was tell them I wouldn't test.

A few weeks later, a coach came in to put me through the wringer. This time, Coach Reid advised me to participate. It was Coach Mark Duffner, the linebacker coach for the Cincinnati Bengals. Coach Duff was about 6'4" and 270 lbs. He had coached at College of the Holy Cross in Massachusetts and received Coach of the Year honors. Coach Reid had known him for years and trusted that he wouldn't work me into the ground. The Bengals had a unique scouting department. Quite simply, they didn't have one because the assistant coaches were in charge of all scouting. It made sense because they would get to look at the players they would coach. However, being an NFL assistant coach while trying to scout every player in the country was a daunting task.

I spent the entire day with Coach Duff. We had breakfast together and he asked me hundreds of questions. After breakfast, we went to campus so he could measure my height and weight. I wore three pairs of socks and used my hand to pull down on the scale as I weighed in.

Coach Duff caught me and said, "Keep your doggone hands on your sides, Marc!"

The Bengals were known for using athletic linebackers with size. Defensive Coordinator Dick LeBeau placed a high priority on each player's football IQ, and it was Duff's responsibility to see if I could process information quickly. He put me through drill after drill. I must have gone through every drill known to man. Coach Duff wanted to see every little strength and weakness on my athletic resume. He made me run at him full speed and then threw a ball at my face as hard as he could. He may have looked like an offensive lineman but he had a rocket for an arm. I dropped a few.

I liked Coach Duff. He had a way of building you up and instilling confidence while he drilled you. What I respected most was that he loved his job. It wasn't work to him. He not only had a strong connection to the game but also to the players he coached. He reminded me a lot of Coach Reid. When we finished, Coach Duff asked me a lot of questions about football and life. He was a great guy and I would have been fortunate to play for him at the next level.

My workouts were done. All the scouts had gotten what they needed to grade a small school kid from Richmond. The scouting report on me was that I was an undersized defensive lineman with the size of a linebacker. I had decent quickness but not good overall speed and I didn't move well in pass coverage. They thought that I could become a productive special teams' player or a middle linebacker. The comparison I heard frequently was to Tedy Bruschi. He was a 240-pound down lineman at the University of Arizona who had been drafted by the Patriots and made the transition to linebacker.

I had done everything in my power and my NFL future was out of my hands. I was praying that one team would believe in me the way that Coach Reid did four years earlier. All I wanted was an opportunity. I knew once I got on the field that I would do everything necessary to make an NFL roster. All it took was for one team to think that I had the goods to play alongside the best athletes in the greatest show on earth. I was projected to be a late-round pick but since I was so hard on myself, I prepared to go undrafted. Even if I was a free agent, all I wanted was the chance to get into an NFL training camp so I could show everyone what I could do.

My life changed forever when the New York Jets selected me in the NFL Draft. Seeing my name scroll across the bottom of that TV screen was the culmination of years of hard work and an exhilarating feeling like no other. After I talked to my mom, Mike, and Mr. Fitz, I sat down and cried. I was only 22 years old but I learned the single most important lesson of my short life: If you put in the hard work, you can achieve anything. I had just been drafted, but my journey was only just beginning.

What people don't realize is that making an NFL team is hard. Getting drafted doesn't guarantee you a roster spot. All the accolades and the awards mean nothing in the NFL. The countless weight lifting sessions, sprints, and grueling practices with Coach Cullen got me to that point. All of that hard work and success only gave me a ticket into the show and a chance to compete. Now I had to prove that I was worthy of staying there. My new life goal became to wear that NFL jersey and run down the field during a regular season game. I still had a long way to go.

WHAT I LEARNED

I have no doubt that most kids who play sports in high school think that they will end up playing in the pros. I did, but I had no idea how difficult it would be. The statistics don't lie. There are roughly 1,086,627 high school football players in the country. Compare that to the 70,147 NCAA football players, and that means only 6.5 percent of high school players make the transition from high school to college football. Of those, only 256 players are drafted and about 300 rookies make an NFL team, which means 1.6 percent of college players make it to the NFL. A mere 150 of those players are in the league for more than four years. Minimum salary after taxes comes to roughly $252,000, which is not enough to live on for the rest of your life. In the end, it's your college education that will provide for you and your family once your football career is over.

CHAPTER 8

WELCOME TO THE NFL

"Talent and good intentions are never enough in this world. You need to be strategic and fearless."

—Robert Greene

One week after the draft, I traveled to the Jets training camp facility located on the Hofstra University campus. My first challenge as draftee would be the three-day rookie mini-camp.

On my arrival, I met with the front office people to sign my contract and fill out the paperwork. I couldn't believe how much was involved. It felt like I was signing my life away and, in a way, that's exactly what I was doing. I was now the property of the New York Jets. NFL contracts are different from most contracts. Many pro sports contracts come with guaranteed money. In the NFL, late-round draftees and free agents aren't given any guaranteed money. You have to survive training camp and actually make the team. Only then will the contract be valid. If you don't make the team, the contract is torn up.

I would still be paid my signing bonus, and after I signed my contract, I was immediately handed the largest check I had ever laid eyes on. Most people would have to work five years to accumulate that sort of wealth. I took the check and walked out of the Jets accounting office backwards. I couldn't believe it was real. I was suddenly being paid to play the game I played for free my entire life. I loved the game and played because I enjoyed the training and combative nature of the sport. To suddenly receive a paycheck for that was difficult to digest.

I drove straight to the bank so I could deposit the check into my account. The female teller took one look at the amount and smiled at me. That was my very first lesson as an NFL player. Money changes people and it changes people's impressions of you. Had I walked in the bank with a check for a couple hundred dollars, that teller would've probably ignored me. It was weird and a little shady. The superficial nature of that exchange stayed with me for a long time.

My next move was a classic rookie mistake: I bought a brand new car. Not just any car but a luxury SUV. Why not? I deserved it. I paid close to $50,000 for a Limited Edition Toyota 4Runner. I could have kept it simple and bought a normal car but no, I had to look like a pro athlete. I hadn't even been in the NFL for a single day and I had already made my first mistake.

I drove back to the facility in my new car to get fitted for my equipment. Once again, I felt like I had won the lottery. At Richmond, I was psyched to get a free T-shirt and a pair of workout shorts. Now I received bundles of T-shirts, warm-ups, and gear. It was an athlete's dream. I was given number 52 and felt elated when I put on the green-and-white colors of the Jets. As I got dressed for my first rookie practice, I realized that I was next to the lockers of All-Pro linebackers Marvin Jones, James Farrior, "Mo" Lewis, and Brian Cox. The four of them and me, a Fall River kid, all in a row. I was awestruck, but I had to shake off that feeling and fast. Once the veterans reported to training camp, I would be one of them so I had to act accordingly.

I knew I faced a challenge but I didn't realize how hard I was about to push myself. This was the NFL. I thought I was strong but everyone was strong. Everyone was fast and everyone had been a superstar. These guys wouldn't be in the league if they weren't.

We had four linebackers in our rookie class. The coaches took us out to the field for another round of testing. We knocked out the vertical leap, pro-shuttle, the 40-yard dash, and then made our way into the weight room for another whack at the 225-pound bench press test. Coach Parcells stood several feet away, watching each of us. That added pressure. Unfortunately, I was tired and only banged out 26 reps. Our second-round pick, Randy Thomas, a guard from Mississippi State, only got six reps. He was well over 300 pounds but lacked weight room strength.

Parcells let him have it, yelling, "Thomas, my grandmother could do more than that!"

I felt bad for him and knew that it was only a matter of time before Parcells laid into the rest of us. We went to our position meetings and began learning the defensive installation. My position coach was Al Groh. He was a tall, frail man with strong football acumen. He had well over 30 years of coaching experience with the Falcons, Giants, Browns, and Patriots before joining the Jets.

I was slotted to play both inside linebacker spots in the Jets 3-4 system. In the 3-4 defense, there are three linemen and four linebackers, typically two outside and two inside. Usually, teams that run a 3-4 defense look for college defensive ends who are too small to play the position in the pros and not quite fluid enough to play outside linebacker in a 4-3 defense. The idea behind the 3-4 defense is to disguise the fourth rusher. Instead of the standard four down linemen in the 4-3, only three players attack on nearly every play. A key for running this defense successfully is having a defensive front of three large defensive linemen who command constant double teams. In particular, the nose tackle must be able to hold ground and occupy several offensive blockers in order to allow the linebackers to make plays. If the defensive lineman can occupy the offensive linemen, that frees up the linebackers to tackle the running back, rush the passer, or drop into pass coverage.

After we finished the installation portion of our meeting, we watched game footage of the Jets linebackers performing their roles with precision. Coach Groh held the video clicker in one hand as he sat in his chair with his leg up on the desk. I had never seen a coach conduct a meeting like that but I wasn't at the University of Richmond anymore. Coach Groh would ask each of us our responsibilities before the snap and none of us wanted to screw that up.

He constantly preached, "Know your job, do your job, know each position's responsibility."

With Patriot teammates, talking shop with The Rock before Monday Night Raw.

Sean Morey, an Ivy League legend, Patriots teammate, and friend.

Off-days meant a huge lunch prepared by my grandma.

My head was spinning. Knowing my job was overwhelming, never mind everyone else's job. I went back to the hotel and fell asleep with my face on my playbook. I was out cold for the rest of the night. After two more days of meetings, position drills and practices, I flew back to Richmond exhausted. I had rookie mini-camp under my belt and knew that I had a while to go before I would see actual game time but I was excited.

Next up was the Rookie Symposium, which was basically an orientation for all 300 drafted rookies. Each team's rookie class was paired with a rookie class from another team. The Jets' rookies were paired with the rookies from the Tennessee Titans. There were presentations, videos, and workshops intended to instruct rookies about NFL history while also promoting wellness, professionalism, and player health and safety. Decision-making, substance abuse, domestic violence, and discrimination were all discussed. Resources also were provided so rookies could successfully identify off-the-field challenges and make the transition from college to the professional level.

For three days, we listened to former NFL players tell stories about making costly mistakes on and off the field. Hall of Famer Cris Carter gave a brilliant speech about his state of mind as a rookie. You could hear a pin drop in the room as he talked about getting caught up in drugs and watching his career spiral out of control. As a young player, he drank heavily and was using cocaine, marijuana, and ecstasy on a regular basis. He failed three drug tests over a three-year period before his coach, Buddy Ryan, finally gave up on him and released him in the summer of 1990. Carter warned us all to stay focused and not let this amazing opportunity pass us by. His speech definitely left a long-lasting imprint on me and influenced my conduct off the field.

After the speeches, individual rookies were called up on the stage and presented with scenarios that required them to make judgment calls on the spot. They later taught us how to put condoms on bananas. That's right, the NFL wanted to teach us how to properly use a prophylactic. Some guys wouldn't do it. Others proudly displayed their finished work. Most of us were fighting to keep our eyes open and counting the minutes until we went home.

Being in the NFL meant you had lots of new fans, including many women. Some women looked at a pro athlete as a meal ticket. Before the symposium started, two beautiful women were sent into the crowd of rookies to socialize with us. Each woman collected as many names and cell phone numbers as possible. When the symposium began, both women walked up on stage and read off the names they collected. The two women then revealed they were HIV positive. We were all speechless. It was a scare tactic that definitely worked. I already knew the importance of hard work and staying humble, but the symposium opened up my eyes to a whole new world that also included the NFL fine system, financial portfolios, stalkers, and the dangers of pain medication.

After the symposium, I returned to Long Island to start Organized Team Activities or OTAs. They were held in late April and early May and were the only practices between the end of the previous season and the start of training camp. I was so excited to get going and start training with my teammates.

It started with daily weight training and conditioning sessions with Head Strength Coach John Lott. We may have been the property of the New York Jets but we belonged to Coach Lott during the off season. At 6'4" and 240 pounds, his presence alone demanded respect. He was a tough but fair coach. I liked how he pushed us to be better and stood over us in the weight room, cuing us in his Texas drawl. A former All-American offensive lineman at the University of North Texas, he played two seasons with the Steelers and the Jets before he was hired by the Jets in 1997 as their strength and conditioning coach.

At the end of OTAs, we were all required to run four 300-yard sprints. We ran 50 yards up and back three times. Each player had to be under a certain time for their position. That may not sound hard but if you hadn't been pushing yourself during the off season, you could be in trouble. A lot of people were nervous but having Coach Lott in our corner definitely stacked the deck in our favor. Coach Lott was known for running all the 300-yard shuttle runs right along with us as we prepped for our conditioning test. That earned him a great deal of respect from the players. He had a very simple set of rules: Don't do anything stupid in the weight room. Never sit during a workout. Push yourself every day. It was his responsibility to get us ready for the rigors of the long NFL season and he took that job seriously.

On the first day of OTAs, I walked into the locker room and all I could hear was a single, booming voice. It belonged to "Mo" Lewis, the biggest linebacker I had ever seen at 6'4" and 270 pounds. I couldn't believe he was a linebacker. Between him and Bryon Cox, who stood 6'4" and 250 pounds, we looked like we had two muscled-up power forwards on defense.

The linebackers were big but their real gift was their speed. Training alongside the Jets' veterans was a humbling experience. They were tough on rookies but I didn't care. I knew it was a rite of passage that all rookies had to endure. During our 350-yard tempo runs around the field, the rookies lined up on the outside so the vets could have the inside lane. No biggie. It was their team. We had to earn their respect and our position on the roster. I did well during weight room training and blew through the conditioning. While at Richmond, Coach Reid ran the hell out of us, so I knew that I could handle anything the NFL coaches could throw at me. When we lifted, we worked hard. When we conditioned, we worked even harder.

I had watched the Jets linebackers excel in the league for years and felt fortunate to have great professionals to guide me. I wanted to learn everything so during film sessions, I studied Marvin Jones, who was named College Football Player of the Year at Florida State University and selected by the Jets as their fourth overall 1993 draft pick. At 6'2" and 250 pounds, his frame was custom built for the position. More important, he was extremely productive and he rarely ever made a mistake. Marvin was quiet around the rookies and didn't say much so I kept my distance and asked questions only when absolutely necessary.

OTAs went by quickly and the 300-yard conditioning test was staring us all right in the face. The coaches placed cones at the 50-yard line. That's where we started. It was six trips to the goal line and back. Assistant Coaches Bill Belichick, Charlie Weiss, Eric Mangini, and Romeo Crennel stood on the goal line to make sure every player touched the line. Coach Parcells stood in the middle of the field so he could see what he'd be working with.

"All you guys better pass the test or, well, you don't want to know," he said.

That didn't make things any easier. We felt his presence the entire time. I certainly didn't want to let him down.

We lined up and, when the whistle blew, we all took off. I ran that test a million times. When I practiced, I always did twice as many reps with half the recovery time so I'd be prepared, but the added pressure of the staff watching over us made me feel like I was running with a weight vest on my back.

When I reached the goal line, Coach Weiss yelled, "Megna you better touch the line and not cut any corners."

Of course, I was going to touch the line. I purposely swiped the white line with my palm so it was visible and didn't leave any doubt. I noticed lots of vets not touching the line and immediately realized it was a rookie thing. After each rep, they gave us a brief rest then repeated the process. Most of us breezed through all four rounds.

Unfortunately, Terry Day, a fourth-round pick from the previous year, fell short on his last run by several seconds. As he neared the finish, he threw his massive body over the goal line. There was complete silence on the field as we all eyed Coach Parcells, who cut Terry on the spot. We never saw him again. I knew Coach Parcells was tough so that didn't surprise me one bit. It confirmed every story I heard about his no-nonsense approach.

With OTAs complete, the next step was training camp at the end of July. Teams often select an outside location, usually a university, to hold at least the first few weeks of training camp. The Jets held their camp at Hofstra University, a school I was already familiar with having been there a few weeks earlier for rookie mini-camp.

New players and coaches used camp to acclimate themselves to the team and the system. For veterans, camp was a time to show the staff that they could still play at a high level. Camp typically began with two-a-days, which were loaded with drills, meetings, weight training, and scrimmaging before the start of the exhibition season with actual preseason games occurring at the very end. Throughout camp, fans got the chance to visit and get an early look at the players. NFL teams created a fan-friendly environment by offering activities and events.

Training camp was an eye-opener for me. The tempo was nothing like we practiced at Richmond. We focused a lot on conditioning in college, but in the pros, they expected you to be in condition. When you're a rookie, you also don't get many reps during drills so when it's your turn you better make the most of that opportunity. And everyone is watching. Rookies are placed under a microscope and everything you do is evaluated. The coaches don't take it easy on you and neither do the players.

Very early on, Bill Parcells told me, "Marc, the veterans are not in the same boat as you. I already know they can play. They just have to show me they can still do it. You're different. You have to show me that you can do what I ask every single day."

Being an NFL rookie is no picnic. Every rookie experiences some sort of hazing. That's the added stress that nobody really accounts for when they come into the league. Most of it is harmless fun between the veteran players and the rookies. However, some moments I could definitely have done without. Veterans would sometimes call out a rookie while eating lunch or dinner, yelling, "Name, school, signing bonus?" After you answered the three questions, you would have to sing your school song or do something equally embarrassing. Those things weren't a big deal but I heard some horror stories. Some rookies would get taped to the goal posts, have their cars parked on the practice field, or be made to take all the guys at their position out to an expensive dinner at a popular steakhouse.

One day before the team meeting on Saturday, Mo Lewis looked over at me and said, "Hey Megs, where are the breakfast sandwiches?"

"What breakfast sandwiches?"

"I told you last night you had to pick up some breakfast sandwiches before the team meeting this morning."

That was bullshit. I knew immediately Mo was testing me. I certainly would not have forgotten something like that but I wasn't in the mood to fight a battle I had no way of winning.

I quickly told Mo, "I'll grab them after the team meeting."

"No, no, little bro. You gotta get 'em now!"

"Now? If I go now, I'll be late for the team meeting."

"You better hurry up then!"

It was 7:15 a.m. and the meeting was in 45 minutes. I knew it was a suicide mission, but I had to try or risk getting hammered even worse by the vets.

Breakfast sandwiches in Hempstead only came from one place: The

Coliseum Deli. All of the guys order the same thing, a dish called "The Gladiator." This thing was a heart attack on a bun. It was loaded with fried eggs, ham, bacon, sausage, scrapple, and cheese. Like that wasn't bad enough, most guys ate two of those things. I couldn't believe it. There I was, trying to call in the order on my phone while speeding down the street in my truck. I didn't think I had a snowball's chance in hell of pulling it off but a miracle happened because when I showed up a few minutes later, all of those sandwiches were bagged and ready to go.

Thank God for hustling New Yorkers who made it possible for me to make it back to the team meeting just seconds before Coach Parcells walked through the door. I still got a dirty look from Special Teams Coach Mike Sweatman but he always looked pissed. I quickly handed out the sandwiches to the veteran linebackers, who scarfed them down in minutes without a single thank you. That was just a small part of my hazing experience with the Jets but it was a cake walk compared to some of the other rookies.

Things didn't get any easier out on the field. I had to prove to everyone that I could play at that level. I worked hard and hoped that it would earn me just a little bit of respect from the vets and coaches but it didn't seem to get me anywhere with them. That was tough because you never knew if you were in the good graces of the staff. I decided to put my head down and hammer through each day's obstacles.

One day after practice, a reporter asked Coach Parcells if the rookies understood the responsibility that came with being a pro.

"No. They don't understand the level of conditioning it takes to play at this level," he said. "They must be strong, they must be fast, and most importantly, they must be in top condition."

"Are any of the rookies prepared the way you need them to be?"

"No, none of them. Actually, one guy is. The Megna kid from Richmond is conditioned. Whoever the strength coach is at Richmond did a great job with that kid."

I saw that in the paper the next day and was shocked. It built my confidence a great deal. I knew I was in great condition, but the fact that Parcells noticed me was a huge compliment. It was actually more of a compliment to the staff at Richmond and their emphasis on strength and conditioning. I was physically prepared but that was just a small piece of the puzzle. Football IQ, and being able to assess formations quickly, was the bulk of the work and I still had some distance to go.

Coach Parcells started every practice off with the same drill—the notorious 3-spot drill. This drill was full contact and involved a defensive lineman or linebacker battling an offensive lineman. The defensive player's job was to shed the offensive lineman and tackle the running back before he could gain any yardage. It was used to simulate his role in the defensive scheme. The head-to-head collisions were extremely intense. During our first practice, veteran linebacker Brian Cox was talking smack to rookie Randy Thomas. We all thought Cox would crush Randy, but Randy fired out and smacked Cox right under his chest plate. He lifted him right off his feet and drove him to the ground. Everyone went crazy! Coach Parcells smiled and blew the whistle. Randy had manhandled one of the best linebackers in the game during his very first rep as a pro. In that moment, we all knew Randy Thomas would be a great player.

When it was my turn, I focused first on my collision with the offensive lineman. Sometimes, I was able to make the tackle but I wanted to make my presence known. It was a "live by the sword, die by the sword" type of drill. It was brutal. After a couple of days, my headaches got so bad I avoided laughing and sneezing. That's what the players called the "brain shakes," and it usually took a couple of days to go away. I started taking Advil before practice.

There was another drill called "inside run," during which I had to go through the guard and clog up the ball carrier's running lane. We were supposed to make contact with the ball carrier and then release him. On my first rep, I made a quick read. I took a line of pursuit behind the offensive lineman and tackled All-Pro running back Curtis Martin to the ground. Coach Parcells didn't mind, but Coach Groh was furious and let me know it.

"Dammit, Megna, don't start doing things your way!" he shouted. "We don't do it your way! We do it our way! This is a 'mind your own business' defensive scheme."

It was embarrassing and I was pissed off. I was no longer at Richmond where effort was appreciated and trumped any errors. I was now a pro, and I had to do everything perfectly or risk sacrificing the integrity of the defense. I knew Coach Groh was right but it was still hard to hear. When I had more time to think about what happened, it really changed my perspective. I knew that I had made a good read. I had a good step. I was fast and I got to the ball. When you're a rookie and you first show up at training camp, you don't really get it. You're trying to learn the playbook and everything moves so fast. Making that play in practice finally gave me the confidence that I could play with those guys. I had the ability. Now I had to do it all the time and show the coaches that I knew what the hell I was doing.

As we got deeper into camp, the daily roster became a revolving door as some players were cut and new ones were brought in. I focused on doing my job and not letting any distractions get in my way. It didn't matter what we were doing or how many reps I was getting; I went as hard as possible. Some of the vets got on me for hustling because it made them look bad. That definitely was not my intention. It's the way I was wired. I was just trying to survive.

Camp was not only hard but it was hot. Dehydration became a problem. We were practicing twice a day so it became difficult to keep my weight up. I ate like a maniac and was still dropping weight. With three weeks left of camp, I was already tired and worn down. I was only 22 years old but it felt like my body had been through a war. Thankfully, one of the vets, Chris Hayes, told me to get intravenous fluids between practices to make sure I was hydrated. That helped me more than I could've predicted. I suddenly felt replenished and ready for more punishment, but I was still making mistakes. Part of the problem was that I hadn't played linebacker since high school so I was still getting used to playing off the line. I wasn't reading the offense as quickly as I needed in order to make plays. It was starting to get to me and I was down on myself. Whenever that happened, I usually went to the weight room, the one place that would allow me to clear my head and release all my frustrations.

One day, I was training between practices when I ran into Coach Parcells. He had just stepped out of the steam room and was dripping with sweat and wearing shorts that looked a few sizes too small.

"Megna, do you know how long training camp is?" he asked.

"It's four weeks, Coach." I was always nervous to talk to him because he was a living legend.

"It's four weeks," he said. "There are three preseason games, 16 regular season games, and playoffs."

"Yes, sir."

"That means this thing is a marathon, not a sprint," he said. "You gotta know when to go hard and when to scale it back, son. If you don't, you're not going to make it. Do your job and know your assignment on every play. By now, you should know when you gotta go full steam ahead."

He was right. The NFL was a war of attrition with a season that was nearly the equivalent of two college football seasons. And football is a collision sport. Each game, a player can put his body through trauma that is the equivalent of being in 60 car accidents. There are only a handful of people in this world built for that. Parcells called it staying power, and most players in my situation don't last. I wouldn't let that happen.

After that conversation, I hit the reset button and approached camp with a completely different mindset. I threw myself into the playbook and drilled myself every night by envisioning different offensive formations lined up across from the defense. If I slowed down for a second, someone was there waiting to replace me. Every day was an all-out war and that's why NFL practice was the hardest thing I've ever done. I didn't know if I would end up making the 53-man roster and I didn't care. I knew there were 31 other NFL teams that would be watching our preseason games and I only needed one of those teams to be interested in order for me to be successful.

One of the things that made camp easier was surrounding myself with some good people. I hung around with offensive lineman J.P. Machado from the University of Illinois. He had a reputation for being tough and dependable. One afternoon, after our second practice of the day, Coach Parcells gathered us all in the middle of the field. He brought J.P. into the circle and asked him where his family would be that evening.

"At home, Coach."

"I want you to call your family tonight and tell them you just made the New York Jets."

That was right before the final cuts to the roster. I was so happy for him.

He was a great guy and a terrific football player. I knew how important it was to him. Positive moments like that made the process more rewarding but there were just as many negative moments.

At the end of one practice, I sat in the locker room across from tight end Johnny Mitchell, who was one of the most athletic tight ends in recent history. He came from a storied college program at University of Nebraska and was the 15th overall pick in the draft. Before I left for the day, Johnny turned to me and said, "I'm outta here."

I'll never forget that moment as I watched one of the best tight ends in the NFL stand up and walk out of the locker room. That lesson hit home. It didn't matter who you were or where you were from. You had to be fully committed or you didn't have a shot. If you're heart wasn't in it, you would get eaten alive.

Right when it felt like camp would never end, the preseason started. Our first game was against the Green Bay Packers. It was hard not to be overwhelmed or star struck when I walked onto an NFL field in my New York Jets uniform. It was preseason but it still felt surreal. Nobody can be prepared for how big that moment is until you run out before 80,000 people. It doesn't matter how cool you think you are, you're going to get anxious. Everyone does. It's so loud and there are so many people. Even some of the guys I knew were warriors didn't want to talk before the game because they were so nervous. It happens to everyone their first year in the league.

Before the start of the game, I crossed paths with Brett Favre as he came over to the sideline to talk with one of our vets. He was a lot bigger than I thought. I had to get my mind right because Coach Groh told me that I'd be getting some reps in the second half. I was excited but incredibly nervous. I kept telling myself that I was just as good as everyone else.

The first half came and went. In the third quarter, I heard Coach Belichick tell Coach Groh to put me in during the next series at one of the inside linebacker spots. Belichick must have seen how nervous I was because he put his hand on my shoulder pad and calmly said, "Relax, it's just football."

Maybe it was just football to him, but for me, I was about to experience the moment I had been waiting for my entire life. He then gave me the defensive call and I hustled onto the field and joined the huddle. I relayed the call. When the huddle broke, I took my spot over the right offensive guard. The crowd had been extremely loud all game while I was on the sidelines but now that I was on the field, I couldn't hear a thing.

I was anxious and jittery for the Packers to snap the ball. I looked into the backfield and saw a familiar face. Fullback Matt Snider had been my house-mate at the University of Richmond. An amazing moment but I couldn't enjoy it because they snapped the ball and ran a toss sweep to the corner in my direction. The play happened fast and I mean FAST! I outflanked the Packers running back, but with three quick steps, he was outside me in the blink of an eye. I took a poor pursuit angle and came underneath the guard instead of through his outside shoulder, which was what we had been taught. I made the play from behind and it appeared to be a great play to the untrained eye, but when I looked over to the sidelines Coach Belichick gave me the death stare. He knew that I had screwed up, and had I not caught the running back from behind, he would've been off to the races. I still couldn't believe how fast it all happened. The speed at the NFL level is something for which nobody can prepare.

I played the remainder of the game and managed to do my job most of the time. I never really went head-to-head with Matt, but playing against each other was a terrific experience. It was a huge accomplishment for both of us, but having two athletes on an NFL field at the same time also spoke volumes for Coach Reid and the University of Richmond. The Packers game, though over so quickly, was an experience for me like no other.

When we went back to work at training camp, my body wasn't feeling that bad. I had recovered nicely. On the field, I made some great plays but knew that there was still a lot that I needed to clean up. With final cuts right around the corner, I wasn't very confident about making the final roster.

The night before final cuts were announced, I packed up all my things. Camp was over so I'd be moving out of the Hofstra dorms either way. I didn't sleep much that night and went over the entire training camp experience in my head. I kept asking myself the same questions: *Did I do enough to earn a spot? Did I have more positive moments or negative moments? Is this the end of my football career? If this is it, what do I do next?* I knew that I wasn't built for an office job. What else could I possibly do?

The coaches started making cuts at 9:00 a.m., so I figured that I'd be safe if I made it past 10:30 a.m. I headed to the cafeteria for breakfast and made the slow walk back to the dorm. By 10:00 a.m., things were looking good, but I left my room half an hour later and bumped right into the "Turk." Turk worked in the player personnel office and was given the thankless job of knocking on players' doors to inform them of their demise.

"I'm sorry, Marc, but Mr. Haley would like to speak with you," he said.

Dick Haley was the head of player personnel. I thought I had made it and was in the clear but Haley apparently thought otherwise. I grabbed my playbook and headed over to the office. Haley told me how I did some positive things in camp and explained how the linebacker positions were extremely competitive but I didn't hear any of what he was saying. All I heard was, "You're not good enough!" He never said those words but that's how I felt.

Haley brought me over to Coach Belichick's office for a talk.

"I think you have the potential to be a good player," Coach Belichick said. "You need more reps at linebacker. If you can catch on with a team and they can allocate you to NFL Europe, it will really help you improve. Whether it's the practice squad or playing in Europe, it will help you gain experience."

He thought I would get picked up by another team and that would give me an opportunity to improve. I appreciated Coach Belichick for taking the time. He was a great coach and I valued his opinion. Several times, he stayed after practice and helped me work on my steps and blitzing from depth. You could see how much he loved to coach. Spending time with a small-school hopeful like me really spoke volumes about his passion for the game. That talk with Coach Bill stayed with me for a long time.

I packed up my truck and drove off campus. I didn't get far before I pulled over and began to cry. I had worked my entire life for that moment and I had just been told I wasn't good enough. I knew that it could be the end of my football days. I felt like I had let my family down. The people of Fall River had been rooting for me to succeed and it felt like I let them down, too. I was low, but I wiped off my tears and got back on the road.

I could have been back in Fall River in three hours but instead I drove seven hours in the opposite direction to the University of Richmond. Richmond had been my home for the past five years and I needed to see a few supportive faces. If there was ever a time for a motivational Jim Reid speech, this was it.

WHAT I LEARNED

Stay humble and pay your dues. Money changes people, and there will always be someone better. I worked my entire life to make it to the NFL, but once I got there, I found myself faced with an entirely new set of challenges and an entirely new set of distractions. The best thing I could do was stay focused and keep doing what had gotten me to that point.

CHAPTER 9

THE NEW ENGLAND PATRIOTS

"There are no shortcuts to any place worth going."

—Beverly Sills

I was in Richmond for less than a day when I received a call from my agent, Jack Mula, who told me the New England Patriots wanted to sign me to their practice squad.

Did I hear him right? The Patriots? I was in shock. Talk about going from the bottom to the top. Not only did I grow up in Massachusetts but the Patriots were my favorite team since I was a boy. When I was in kindergarten, they videotaped us saying what we wanted to do when we grew up. Even at that age, there was never any doubt about what I wanted: "I'm going to play football for the New England Patriots!"

In August 1999, it actually happened! It was a dream come true for me and it happened only one day after it felt like I hit rock bottom. Things can change that fast and I couldn't have asked for a better outcome because there wasn't a team in the league for which I would rather play. If someone had told me one week earlier that I was going to get cut by the Jets and wind up on the Patriots, I would have told them to cut me immediately. Those two days were an emotional roller coaster for me, but the story of my NFL career up to that point was not an uncommon one.

So, what exactly is the practice squad? I didn't know at first, but in addition to the 53-man roster, each NFL team can keep eight players on its practice squad. Those eight players are typically rookies like me who are cut during training camp, or others who are on the cusp of making a roster. I wasn't playing in any games. I wasn't even suiting up, but I was still an official member of the team. There were definitely worst places I could be.

Technically, I was still a free agent so I could be signed to a team's regular roster at any time throughout the season. NFL teams are free to poach players from another team's practice squad without having to compensate the team. To me, this was another opportunity. I just needed a chance. I needed to get my foot in the door. Once I got on the field, I was confident that the Patriots would add me to the roster. I wasn't going to waste the opportunity.

I couldn't wait to get back to New England. The next morning, I packed up my truck and headed North on I-95 to Foxboro, the home of the New England Patriots. I must have driven 1,300 miles in two days.

When I arrived at the facility, Bobby Grier, the head of player operations, was there to meet me at the door. We went up to his office and I signed my contract. Head Coach Pete Carroll popped in.

"Welcome to the New England Patriots," he said, shaking my hand.

I went down to get fitted for my equipment. I was so excited that I felt like a little kid. I was given number 96 because I was the last linebacker brought in. The number choices were slim pickings but I certainly wasn't going to complain.

It was time to hit the field. I was literally jumping right into the fray. I made my way over to the locker room and got dressed alongside the rest of the Patriot linebackers. That wouldn't have been a big deal for most NFL rookies but when you grow up in Massachusetts and your locker is directly across from Willie McGinest, Tedy Bruschi, and Chris Slade, it's a big moment. I had watched those guys play on TV for years.

The whole day had been surreal, but I couldn't revel in it too long because now I had to play. Practice started with light drills. I joined the rest of the linebacker core that included Ted Johnson, Marty Moore, Andy Katzenmoyer, and Vernon Crawford. I may have been wearing a Patriots uniform and was out there practicing with some of my sports heroes but I knew that I hadn't made it yet. I had a long way to go.

The practice squad guys didn't get much respect from the staff. That bothered me because respect meant a great deal to me. What bothered me even more was having to watch new guys at my position show up at practice every single day.

Slade used to joke about it with me all the time, saying, "Hey Marc, your buddies are here."

"What?" At first, I didn't get it.

"Those are the guys who are trying to take your job."

He was right. Not only were they all blue-collar white kids from small schools who were the same size and had the same haircut as me but they were all chomping at the bit for the chance to wear my jersey.

I was literally the last guy on the roster. If there was an injury at another position or the team needed to move people around on the roster to make room, they would release me. I needed to give them a reason not to. Every day I had to convince the team that I belonged there. Coach Reid and Coach Cullen ran us harder at Richmond, but in the NFL, I had to practice hard every day in order to keep my job. That's why I flew around like a madman during practice. I went into every practice as if someone was trying to rip my dream away from me. That was a lot of pressure. Every player in the NFL feels pressure but the vets could approach practice differently. They had to be in the right place at the right time but they had already earned their way onto the roster. The coaching staff knew what to expect from the vets on game day so those guys could go half speed.

When it came to the practice squad players, the coaching staff expected three things: 1) always know where you're supposed to be, 2) keep your mouth shut, and 3) give insane effort.

Luckily for me, all three of those things were second nature. Playing for Jim Reid at Richmond, we didn't have the choice to play any other way. I brought that same energy to the Patriots practice squad. I played hard because I didn't want to give the coaching staff a reason to say, "He's complacent. Let's replace him." I also knew that I couldn't play scared or play only not to screw up. I had to stand out in a positive way. I may have been one injury away from getting cut but I was also one injury away from making the team. If a linebacker went down, they'd bump one of the linebackers from special teams over to play linebacker and then move one of the practice squad guys to special teams. It happens that quickly so I had to be ready and I had to prove myself.

Each week, our job on the practice squad was to play the role of the opposing team's defense and prep the offense for different strategies they might face. I went back and forth between linebacker and defensive end. The pressure might have been through the roof but it certainly felt great to be out there. The icing on the cake for me was the chance to practice against Drew Bledsoe. After being drafted out of Washington State by the Patriots as first pick in the 1993 NFL Draft, Bledsoe was destined for greatness. Not only did he have a rocket for an arm but he was a great size for a quarterback and had already shattered multiple NFL records. I loved watching him practice because he made it look so simple. I don't know how many times I saw him thread a needle and complete a pass to a receiver in double coverage.

In practice, the defenders were told not to go anywhere near Drew. If we beat our blockers, we were supposed to run right by him. They didn't even want us to lower our heads because he might hit his hand on a helmet when following through on a pass. That's easier said than done when battling on the field. On one play, I beat the offensive lineman but he turned around and pushed me in the back. I vaulted right into Drew. The entire practice went silent. You could hear a pin drop. Everyone looked at me as if I committed a mortal sin. Luckily, Drew wasn't hurt. Coach Carroll immediately pulled me out and sent a message by keeping me off the field for the rest of the day.

After practice, Coach Carroll would put some of us through more drills to give us extra reps. Some players thought it was a pain in the ass but I welcomed it because it gave me the chance to spend more time learning from one of the greatest players in franchise history, Andre Tippett, now a linebacker coach for the team. Not only was he my personal sports hero growing up but he played in five Pro Bowls, was named to the 1980s All-Decade Team, and would later be elected to the NFL Hall of Fame in 2008. He held the Patriots franchise record for quarterback sacks with 100. Even after he retired, he remained active and earned an advanced Black Belt in martial arts. His physique was impressive and he had huge hands. He made me look like a small child when I stood next to him.

During those sessions, I also got to go one-on-one with tight end Kerry Taylor, who won a National Championship at the University of Massachusetts. He was a great tight end who ran terrific routes. I wasn't used to covering players his size in pass coverage so I was in over my head at times, but it helped me work on my weak spots. We had some absolute battles. I loved every minute of it and Kerry became one of my closest friends on the team.

I was playing well and making an impression on the coaches and the players, but the veteran linebackers made sure not to let any of it go to my head. Those guys gave me a hard time, especially Tedy. He refused to call me by my first name. It was always "rookie" or just "rook." I received my fair share of hazing but I didn't mind it. It never got too bad because I was only on the practice squad. I usually had to carry equipment and buy breakfast donuts. No big deal.

There was one time when I got some heat and rubbed the vets the wrong way. The most popular hazing ritual was the position dinner. That's when all the players at a particular position went out for an expensive dinner at a top-of-the-line restaurant. The vets order everything on the menu and do their best to run up the tab. You name it, they order it. The catch is that the rookies have to pick up the bill and there isn't anything they can do about it. For our position dinner, the veteran linebackers chose The Capital Grille in Providence, Rhode Island. It was by far one of my favorite restaurants and I had been there a few times. It certainly wasn't cheap.

Tedy Bruschi made sure to tell me and Andy Katzenmoyer that we would be responsible for the bill. Andy was a first-round draft pick and made a lot more money than me, so earlier in the week before the dinner, he told me not to go. That way I wouldn't have to split the bill. That was incredibly kind of him. I really dodged a bullet because splitting that bill would have crushed me. Tedy still believed every rookie had to pay his dues, however. He put some extra pressure on me for a while but those guys on our linebacker crew were great. They always knew when to cut you some slack.

I quickly settled in with the team and fell into a routine. I rented a small apartment in North Attleboro only minutes away from the stadium so I could roll out of bed and be at practice in minutes. The location was perfect. The inside was a little sparse. I had a futon and a large TV. That was about it. I've always been a minimalist. The thought of having too much clutter overwhelmed me so I kept things simple. Nobody would have believed that a professional athlete lived in that small studio. I had some kitchenware but I didn't do much cooking and typically went out to eat. One of my favorite spots was the Outback Steakhouse right by Foxboro Stadium. Back in college, I didn't have a dime to my name so it felt like a treat when I went out to a restaurant. Now that I had cash on me at all times, I could look at a menu without worrying about cost. Circumstances had changed quite a bit.

The best thing about playing for the Patriots was that I was still close to Fall River and I went home to see my mother and brother every chance I got. They were always there for me, so I wanted to do everything I could to repay them. We made a rule to go out to eat once a week and catch up on everything. When Mr. Fitz joined us, we traveled in a pack of four and hit up some of the local spots like the Liberal Club and Tweet Balzano's. No matter where we ended up, my brother and I always ordered way too much food and left feeling sick.

It was great to get away from football for a little while but my mind was never far from the game. Whether on the field or not, you could feel the energy build up during the week as game day approached. At this point in my career, game day was a little different. Inactive players were allowed to be on the sidelines, but practice squad players had to watch the games from the stands. We all got tickets and sat together. That was rough. Actually, it was a nightmare. It was hard to sit in the stands and watch while the other guys played but I tried to make the best of it. For away games, we basically had a free weekend. I'd get together with some of the other guys to watch the game, but it was an opportunity for us to either take some time off or do some extra training.

Monday was a short installation practice and film day. Tuesday was our day off but I always used Tuesday as an extra workout day. I'd go over to the facility to train with Johnny Parker, our strength coach. We'd lift weights and he'd put us through his brutal treadmill sessions. The smart thing would have been to let my body recover the rest of the day but that would have been too easy. Instead, I drove over to Fall River to run the hills at North Park. I gave everything I had, and it took about 12 trips up and down those hills before my legs were fried and I called it a day.

After my marathon workout, I'd meet up with my brother and we'd head over to my grandparent's house in the South End for an Italian lunch. My grandma made the most amazing sauce to go with her pasta, meatballs, chicken cutlets, and garlic bread. It was a feast. My grandparents were so excited to have me and my brother over and I loved spending time with them. Life as a rookie wasn't easy and it definitely wasn't glamorous but my family made it manageable.

Luckily, I also had some pretty great teammates. I grew close to the linebackers. They gave me a hard time but they also looked out for me. One of my best friends on the team ended up being my old high school rival, Sean Morey. Sean was the Massachusetts native I had played against at Durfee and last saw at the Hula Bowl. He had been drafted by the Patriots in the seventh round. We gravitated toward each other immediately because we were both blue-collar kids who were told every step of the way that we weren't good enough, big enough, or fast enough to play. Yet, there we were on the New England Patriots. We also made the same mistakes. We both made the awful decision to buy the exact same 4Runner when we got drafted. Sean's was green. Mine was silver.

Sean, Kerry, and I became really close and we had our share of fun when we went out on the town. Foxboro was the perfect location because we were close to both Boston and Providence. If we wanted to go to Providence, we'd hit up The Capital Grille for dinner. Sean went to Brown so he'd take us out on the town. It felt like we were out with the mayor of Providence. No matter what we did, we always ended the night at the same place—Spike's Junkyard Dogs. They had a hotdog named after Sean called the All-American. If we wanted to go in the other direction and head to Boston, we'd usually meet up with my college roommate, Elio. His family owned a pizza place called Tony's in West Roxbury. We'd stop there before heading into the city. We may not have been on the Patriot's game-day roster but we were always recognized and given lots of attention whenever we went out. I don't think any of us were really ready for that.

Even though I wasn't a star, playing in the NFL definitely gave me a degree of special access. One Monday after practice, running back Kevin Faulk invited a couple of the guys on the team to a WWF event at the Worcester Centrum. He rented a couple of limos for the trip. When we arrived, we were escorted to the locker room. I had been up since 5:00 a.m. that day and was exhausted so I sat down on a folding chair. As soon as I sat down, I heard a loud voice scream "You're in The Rock's chair, son!"

I jumped up and found myself face-to-face with the man himself: Dwayne "The Rock" Johnson. He started laughing and said, "Sit down, man. Do you think I really talk like that? I was just playing."

The Rock may have been the biggest draw in the WWF but he was a normal guy who worked hard for his success. He wanted to be a football player and played defensive line at the University of Miami but fell short of the NFL. He finished out his career in the Canadian Football League before turning to wrestling and making it to the top. He was not only one of the coolest guys in the business but it turned out that he was just like us—a normal kid who worked hard for his success. We shared the same energy and enthusiasm. You could tell that he had that never-ending desire to make his dreams come true. We talked for an hour about wrestling, football, and training. He even swapped our tickets out for front row seats and handed us all T-shirts.

During the main event, things got pretty heated between The Rock and his opponent. At one point, he picked up the other guy and launched him over the first-row railing and into my lap. After the match, The Rock called all of the Patriots players into the ring to sing his famed "Smackdown Hotel" theme song. The whole thing was surreal. I had grown up watching Hulk Hogan and Andre the Giant. Never did I think I'd find my way into a professional wrestling ring. But there I was, standing in the middle of the ring with ten of my teammates, hanging out with The Rock. My mom and brother were watching at home and couldn't believe what was happening. That was, without a doubt, a bucket list moment for this kid from Fall River.

No matter what happened at night, we were always ready for practice the next day. The second you walked into the Patriots facility you had to be on. That was true for the vets and it was true for the practice squad guys as well.

As we reached the home stretch of the season, it started to look like I wasn't going to get my shot at the active roster. That changed on December 7 when Coach Carroll called me into his office.

"Marc, we're going to add you to the 53-man roster for the last four games of the season," he said. "You've worked your ass off and you've earned it."

I couldn't have been happier. "Thank you, Coach, I will not let you down."

That was the news I had been waiting to hear, but what I didn't anticipate was the amount of pressure that came with it. I had more than the weight of my own expectations on my shoulders. I was carrying the weight of Fall River, Richmond, and every boy who ever dreamed big and was told no.

Practice was intense that week as I prepared for my new role against the Indianapolis Colts. On Saturday morning, we were off to Indianapolis. It was my first time traveling with a pro team. We all met at Foxboxo and everybody was dressed in their best (or at least their most colorful) suit. As we boarded a bus to Logan Airport, I was given a crash course in fashion from Larry Whigham, who wore flashy red pinstripes.

Once at the airport, we drove straight onto the runway. It was pretty cool to skip check-in and all the security lines. It was a quick flight to Indianapolis and a short bus ride to the hotel. Unless you paid $75 for your own room, you were paired with a teammate. I shared a room with linebacker Andy Katzenmoyer. He knew it was my first time traveling with the team so he looked out for me.

As I got settled in, there was a knock on the door. One of the assistant coaches pulled me aside to tell me that that I'd been deactivated for tomorrow's game. It felt like a punch to the stomach. My dream would be delayed yet again. I was crushed but made my peace and I tried to enjoy the rest of the trip. I wasn't allowed to dress for the game, but deactivated players were allowed to stand on the sidelines. The Patriots ended up losing to the Colts 20-15, but my first trip on the road with an NFL team was still an unforgettable experience.

The next few weeks were more of the same and I was deactivated for all of the remaining games. It was devastating but I kept doing my job. At the end of the season, Coach Carroll spoke to the team. The mood in the locker room remained light. The season didn't turn out like we had hoped, but everyone worked hard and we all looked forward to some much-needed rest. We had to clean out our lockers. Players returned their workout clothes and practice gear. The equipment staff placed large bins in the middle of the locker room for all the cleats. I kept a couple pairs for my off-season workouts.

It felt like years had gone by since I had been drafted. I couldn't believe that it had only been one season. It was disappointing that I never got into a game, but before I left the facility that day, I made sure to think about how far I had come and how much I had accomplished. I was proud but I wasn't content. That day I made a promise to myself that I would not stop until I ran down that field wearing the Pats blue. I knew that was going to make me want to work harder than ever. It was less about football and more about finishing what I started. I needed to see my journey through until the end. Pauline Megna did not a raise a quitter.

In the spring, the Patriots organization underwent a major change. News of Coach Carroll's firing flooded the media and the speculation began about who would replace him. At the same time, 200 miles away in New York, my former team the Jets were experiencing their own growing pains. Head Coach Bill Parcells was about to step down and rumors circulated about his defensive coordinator, Bill Belichick, making the move to the Patriots to become their head coach.

I knew Coach Belichick from my short time with the Jets, and the possibility of having him as the Pats' head coach was terrific. Coach Belichick was the only coach who spent time with me after practice when I was struggling during training camp. Coach Belichick was also the only staff member who spoke to me before I was released by the Jets. I respected him a great deal. However, when Parcells stepped down as head coach of the Jets, he had already arranged with team management to have Belichick succeed him. That lasted one day. After his hiring was announced, Belichick took the podium to announce his resignation from the Jets. He was then introduced as the next head coach of the New England Patriots. Since he was still under contract with the Jets, NFL Commissioner Paul Tagliabue ruled that the Patriots had to give the Jets a first-round draft pick in 2000.

Robert Kraft gave Coach Belichick near complete control over the team's football operations. He was basically the general manager as well. We could immediately feel the energy begin to shift within the organization. Coach Belichick was known to clean house, so it was no surprise when he went right to work hiring and firing. Much to our surprise, he let go of long-time strength coach Johnny Parker and quickly replaced him with veteran Mike Woicik. Rob Ryan was hired as linebacker coach and legendary New York Giants linebacker Pepper Johnson was brought on to assist. Charlie Weiss came over from the Jets and Brad Seely became the new special teams' coach. With all the players and coaches being moved around, I expected him to get rid of me as well but that didn't happen. He saw potential in me and I didn't want to disappoint.

While the Pats revamped their staff, Sean Morey, Kerry Taylor, and I were working on our own physical development. One area we knew that we could all improve was our speed and quickness. That's what separated the good players from the great players in the NFL. We took it upon ourselves to hire Mike Morris, the Patriots' former assistant strength coach. Mike was the brother of New York Giants' running back Joe Morris and a former track star who specialized in speed development.

On Mondays, Wednesdays, and Fridays, the three of us met with Mike at the YMCA in Taunton. Those speed sessions were brutal. I hadn't endured that kind of abuse since I played for Coach Reid at Richmond. You'd think that I would be more accustomed to that type of training as a pro but that wasn't the case. Mike was relentless. He subjected us to a whole new level of pain, but eventually I felt like I could run for days.

Training for the NFL is all about speed, strength, and mobility. A good comparison is to think of college football players as weightlifters trying to play pick-up basketball, while NFL players are like basketball players who can lift a lot of weight. The league caters to athletes. A guy like Richard Seymour was a 6'6" and 315-pound defensive tackle, but size was not his number one asset. It was his speed. That's what makes the NFL players extraordinary.

At Richmond, weight lifting was 60 percent of my training routine and conditioning was 40 percent; in the NFL, lifting was 30 percent and track work was 70 percent. We trained like sprinters and that's how they made us fast. There was meticulous attention to detail. I was doing hip drills and firing my knees while making sure to have proper elbow drive, posture, and even hand position while sprinting. That was much different from the straight survival approach to basic sprints we did at Richmond. We may have lifted less frequently but the programs were more efficient so we got stronger in less time. If I were to go back to college and utilize all the sprint and mobility work I learned in the NFL, it would have made me a much better player and a much better athlete.

Going into a new season, it didn't matter how much time you spent in the weight room or how conditioned you were because when they snapped that ball for the very first time in practice, you were out of shape. Weight room shape and track shape are different from being in actual football shape. When you have a helmet and shoulder pads on, it changes everything. The mechanics of running are completely different. If you haven't been wearing pads during the off season, it's going to feel awkward and uncomfortable when you return to practice. One of the biggest insults in football is to call somebody a workout warrior. Teams would rather have a guy who is weak in the weight room but an absolute baller on the field. It does no good if you can bench and squat heavy if that doesn't translate to results on the field. Strength is important but it's about more than lifting weights. It's about training your body so you can perform.

I approached my off season workouts like I had four months to train for a marathon. If you're training to run a marathon, you're not going to start running 20 miles the first day. The marathon in my case was the football season, so I wanted to build myself up over time and not do too much too soon. I didn't rush. I focused on micro-progressions to make sure that I hit my sweet spot at the start of the season and could sustain that same level of performance over the next couple months. The workouts in that program were timely, organized, and strategic, and Sunday was always a max-effort day. The point was to mentally prepare myself for the serious psychological effort required on Sundays during the regular season.

No matter how hard you train, there are some things that you can never control. Shortly after Belichick joined the team, he called me into his office.

I felt comfortable speaking with Coach Bill because of my past experiences with him, but I had no idea what was happening. *Was I in trouble? Was I about to be cut? Was I falling short of their expectations?*

I knocked on the door and Coach Bill looked up.

"Take a seat, Marc," he said.

"Yes, sir," I was always ridiculously polite when addressing my coaches over the years, another habit Coach Reid drilled into my head at Richmond. I wasn't going to change and turn into Joe Cool in front of Bill Belichick.

"I like the way you work, Marc," he said. "Your work ethic will give you a chance in this league. What you need is more experience at linebacker."

That's usually the point in the conversation when the coach butters you up before saying, "We're letting you go." But that's not what happened. In fact, I could have never predicted what he was going to say next.

"I'm sending you to NFL Europe," he said. "You've been allocated to the Barcelona Dragons so you can work on your skills and become a better linebacker."

At the time, NFL Europe was like the AAA baseball of the NFL, and their season began once the NFL season ended.

"You're gonna like it over there, but you have to stay focused and be careful because it's a lot of fun."

"Yes, sir," I said.

"Get ready because you leave in a couple weeks."

I left that office not knowing what to think. The only time I had been out of the country was when I went to Canada for a hockey tournament as a kid. I knew nothing about Europe. I wasn't exactly well traveled so Barcelona was going to be a big change. I had no idea what was in store for me.

Sean Morey got the same talk from Coach Belichick and had been allocated to Barcelona as well. It was good to have a friend traveling with me, but we weren't on the team yet. NFL Europe had their own training camp in Orlando. That was where we would practice and be evaluated by the Barcelona coaching staff.

There was one big catch: When you were allocated to a European team, you had to make the roster. If you got cut during training camp for NFL Europe, they'd cut you from the NFL team as well. It was a do-or-die situation and it came with a ton of pressure.

Getting ready for kickoff

My first sack as a Patriot.

Punt coverage

"Please hold onto the ball!"

WHAT I LEARNED

Have patience and enjoy the process. Success doesn't happen overnight. There will be setbacks and disappointments along the way. But if you keep your eye on the prize and continue to work hard, you will eventually get something positive out of the experience, even if it's not what you initially expected.

CHAPTER 10

NFL EUROPE

"It isn't all about talent. It's about dependability, consistency, and being able to improve. And again, if you work hard and you are coachable, and you understand what you need to do, you can improve."

—Bill Belichick

I boarded a plane from Logan Airport to Orlando for two weeks of scrimmages. Cuts were made daily and it always felt like it could happen to me at any moment, but I played well and did enough to make the roster. Both Sean and I became the newest editions to the Barcelona Dragons.

The next thing I knew, I was on a plane to San Francisco to join the rest of the NFL Europe hopefuls in a mass evaluation. We were all taken to a large convention center. It felt like the combine as they measured our height, weight, and even our hand size. We were screened for drugs and then given written tests with a series of bizarre questions like, "Do you take pleasure in beating animals?" They were looking for psychological flaws, personality disorders, and dysfunctional issues that could put their team and franchise in a compromising position. It felt as if we were being treated like cattle but that was the NFL.

With testing complete, we were off to Europe for what would be the experience of a lifetime. There must have been 200 athletes on my flight. It was an entire plane filled with disruptive passengers blasting music, drinking, partying, and even dancing in the aisles. I'm pretty sure most of them had never been to Europe. Some got drunk so fast that they fell asleep and woke up hurting for the remainder of the ten-hour flight. I listened to music, read, and wrote some notes in my journal. I started documenting my athletic career in high school so someday I would be able to share my experiences with my family and friends.

Once in Spain, we were bused to Sitges, a town about 35 kilometers southwest of Barcelona, which was renowned for its beaches, nightspots, and historical sites. The NFL put us up in a hotel located right on the Mediterranean coast. It was a great spot. From the hotel, you could watch the sunset over the ocean. Some nights, it was absolutely breathtaking.

On our first night, we experienced a traditional Spanish dinner. Finally, a real meal. The tables at the hotel were loaded with salad, steaks, and a giant-sized pan holding a mountain of paella. That was Spain's national dish and it would be my go-to meal for the next several months. They also offered us sangria. That was not the smartest move by the hotel staff.

Before I left New England, the offensive line coach pulled me aside and told me that they were sending a lineman with us.

"I want you to keep an eye on him and keep him out of trouble," he said.

On our first night in Barcelona, that lineman drank a little too much and got into an altercation with a few guys on the team. The next day, he was on a plane home. Let's just say, the hotel made some modifications after the first night. This is the reason why there is no alcohol on any NFL tables. Some guys can't handle it and the team doesn't want to put players in that situation.

One thing I noticed immediately about Spain was the women. Women in America were conservative compared to the women we met there. On my first night, a girl looked at me and said, "Come home with me. I have a very big bed." *Did she just say what I think she said?* I knew right then that I had to pay close attention to what was going on and what was being said because things were very different.

The next morning, we woke up to what sounded like a giant block party. I opened my shutter doors to see the streets packed with people dancing, drinking, and living it up. I couldn't believe there was that much activity going on right outside my door. It wasn't even the weekend. Living there was going to be a challenge. I wasn't against having fun but I was there to better my chances for next season in the NFL and I didn't want to let a party stand in my way. I was willing to hold off on the hijinks until the season was over. I was there to play, and luckily, we dove right in and started immediately.

The head coach of the Barcelona Dragons was Jack Bicknell. He was like John Wayne. His love of country music and horseback riding got him the nickname "Cowboy Jack." He had been the head coach at Boston College for nine years and led Heisman Trophy winner Doug Flutie past the Miami Hurricanes in the 1984 Cotton Bowl. Coach Bicknell had been the coach of the Barcelona Dragons for the past ten years and assembled a staff of experienced coaches who knew football inside and out. Every player in Europe wanted to play in Barcelona because of Cowboy Jack.

There are two types of coaches. There are the tough coaches who want to bang every day and put you through brutal practices. Then there are the coaches who know the game wears you down and want to save your body so they take it easy on you. Cowboy Jack was one of the guys who liked to take it easy. He understood that most of us had just gone through rookie mini-camp, NFL off-season mini-camp, training camp, and an entire NFL season before taking a month off and arriving in Europe to play another full season. He knew we had to take it easy on our bodies or we'd fall apart. He treated us like pros and expected us to act like pros, but his practices were another level of easy.

On a typical day, we woke up at 7:00 a.m. and had something to eat. We met at 8:00 a.m. to watch film for a half hour then get on a bus to arrive at practice by 9. Most days, we practiced only in helmets and shoulder pads. Other days were just a walk-through without contact. Either way, practice was over at 10:15 a.m. It was good because we were rested and went into games fresh, but you also need that contact during the week to really be ready. A little balance between contact and no-contact probably would have been better, but he was a veteran coach who knew what he was doing so I respected his approach.

One of the biggest challenges was to figure out what to do with the rest of our day once we got back to the hotel. Some of us worked out at this little place called The Barn, which was literally a barn. Not an exaggeration. Cows and goats wandered around outside. I had never seen anything like it, but the gym left something to be desired. Inside, they had one bench press, a couple of 45-pound plates, a couple of dumbbells, and a squat rack. I worked out for an hour or so and then ate lunch, and still I had the rest of the day free. If we had a day off, guys took a plane to Ibiza for a night and came back the next day. We all had our fun but we made sure we were ready for the games.

The league in Europe was much different than the NFL. There were only six teams: Barcelona, Rhein, Scotland, Amsterdam, Frankfurt, and Berlin. We played every team twice during the 10-game season. Everyone playing on a roster in Europe was an NFL prospect and jockeying to be one of the few guys who was going to make it. The players were technicians. They all played really well and never made a mistake so the competition was always tough.

I did a little bit of everything that season. I was on special teams and I played almost every down on defense. I was pass rushing on third down. I did it all. The real benefit of playing in Europe was being able to play real football again. I had been on the practice squad, which was not the same as playing in real, live games. When the season began in Barcelona, it felt like I had taken a year off from football. I was finally back in the mix and battling out there on the field. More important, I was gaining experience as a linebacker.

The games weren't any less physical than they were in the NFL. We all got banged up. Everyone knows football is a violent game but no pro would ever play a single down if they stopped to acknowledge every injury. Somebody is getting hurt on every snap. The injuries pro football players fight through are injuries that would prevent the average guy from going to work for a week. I was lucky enough never to have been sidelined with an injury but I suffered my share of bumps and bruises.

I was on the kickoff team for one of the first games of the year against the Rhein Fire of Germany. Playing in front of a packed crowd, I felt my adrenaline pumping. Once the ball was kicked, I sprinted 40 yards down the field as fast as I could and lowered my head into an offensive lineman who was twice my size. Smack! We hit helmet-to-helmet and both went down.

I got up and walked back to the sideline where I watched the next play. Dan Collins, who also was from Massachusetts and went to Boston College, came up to me looking concerned. He asked, "Marc, what are you doing?"

I had no idea what he was talking about. It turns out that Dan played for Rhein and I was on the wrong sideline. Not only was I on the wrong sideline but I was supposed to be in the game. My vision was blurry. I couldn't see straight and I was light on my feet. I tried to blink my eyes a few times hoping that it would go away but it didn't. I couldn't take myself out of the game so I had to fight through it.

For the rest of the game, I figured out a way to adapt so I wouldn't embarrass myself. I loosened up my alignment and tried to cheat when I thought a play was going in a particular direction. I wasn't as sharp as I usually was so I had to do things to make sure I was putting myself in proper position and not causing gaping holes in the defense.

Back then, we didn't know what we do now about concussions. There was speculation but there wasn't yet evidence of long-term damage. Still, those injuries weren't ignored. It was a huge deal to the training staff. It didn't matter if I was playing for Barcelona or for the Patriots; if I came out of the game, there was no guarantee that I'd ever get back in. I didn't want to put myself on their watch list so I kept injuries like that to myself and tried to push through. That was difficult because a severe concussion could linger for weeks. Even if you start to feel okay, one hit can leave your head ringing again.

The week following the Rhein game, I tried to deal with it on my own and avoid any brutal contact in practice. Luckily, Jack Bicknell's light practices helped me recover and get ready for the next game.

I played well in the next game and the rest of that season. And I played a lot. By the end of the year, I had played about 90 percent of the snaps on defense and finished the season second on the team in tackles. We had a mediocre year but it didn't matter to the people of Barcelona at all. They still went crazy and threw us a huge party in the streets. It was insane. I went out that night with Sean Morey and we were all over the city.

My time in Barcelona was incredible. The people of Spain were the first to chip away at the confrontational attitude that I developed growing up in southeastern Massachusetts. Their attitude and energy was completely different from anything I had ever experienced. They genuinely wanted to be your friend and help in any way possible.

One night, I asked an older man in his sixties where he bought his signature FC Barcelona Football Club shirt. He took it off and handed it to me. I didn't even know the guy and he was offering up his favorite team's jersey. It caught me off guard. I assumed that he wanted something in return, but no, that was just the attitude of the Spanish people. Living in Barcelona really opened my eyes and made me realize that there was a great big world out there that was pretty awesome. I got to live in an incredible city, experience a completely different culture while representing the NFL, and be paid to play the game I loved. I didn't want to leave because I was having so much fun but I couldn't stick around to enjoy it. I had to keep my eye on the prize and the prize was making the roster for the New England Patriots.

Training camp was right around the corner. The week I returned from Barcelona, I had to do a conditioning test for the Patriots. I was in shape because I had just played an entire season of football, but I was still a little nervous because I knew that if I weren't ready, Belichick would cut me on the spot. That's just the way that he did it. He was always watching. Every time I made a mistake, I knew that he would be right there to remind me, "Come on, Marc! It's not fucking William & Mary we're getting ready to play."

One of the bad things about Barcelona was the food. Portions were small and the hotel didn't provide me with enough food needed to maintain a 245-pound frame. I was constantly hungry. Combine that with playing football and training and my weight had dropped to 220 by the time I got home. I had to put on weight if I expected my body to take a pounding during training camp. I knew that once I started eating and lifting weights, it would be easy to do that. Still, for the conditioning test, Sean Morey and I decided to practice for two days before we did the real thing.

Everyone on the team had to run 20 sprints. Offensive linemen and defensive linemen had to run 40-yard sprints. Defensive backs and wide receivers had to run 60-yard sprints. Linebackers, fullbacks, and tight ends had to run 50-yard sprints. I ran with the linebackers, which meant that we had to finish each sprint in under six seconds and only got 45 seconds of rest between each rep.

When it was time to go, I lined up between Willie McGinest and Greg Spires from Florida State. Greg looked over at me and asked, "Is this going to be hard for you?"

"Nah, it's not going to be hard," Willie McGinest chimed in, laughing. "Tell him why, Marc."

"Because I'll die out here if I have to."

And I would. Luckily, it didn't come to that.

After eight sprints, Belichick looked over at me and asked, "You aren't tired, are you?"

"Of course not," I said, taking off again for another 50-yard sprint.

That was a huge compliment coming from Coach Belichick. He knew that I would be in excellent shape. A little bit of sugar from Coach Belichick went a long way because it didn't happen often.

With the conditioning test complete, the team headed to training camp at Bryant College in Smithfield, Rhode Island. I had an outstanding camp. I even got some attention from the fans because I was a local guy. A lot of people knew me. My teammates also were great. Chris Slade and Willie McGinest took me under their wing. They didn't have to but they did. The funny thing was by that point in my career, camp wasn't as hard as it was the first time. I knew what I was doing. I also knew the system and that gave me the confidence that I previously lacked. After surviving four years with Jim Reid and Joe Cullen literally running us into the ground, I felt like I could handle anything the NFL coaches threw at me.

The preseason games were my chance to shine and prove myself to everyone. I knew my assignments forward and backward. More important, I got playing time. I had a good chance of making the final roster when I suited up for the Patriots against the Carolina Panthers. It was only a preseason game but it was an important one because it would determine those final roster spots. During the first half of the game, I was playing linebacker when I got drilled by a pulling guard right in the back. The blow completely knocked the wind out of me. The pain in my kidneys was so intense that my eyes watered. Even my teammates could tell that I was hurting.

At halftime, I stepped to the urinal and all that came out was blood. Normally, alarm bells would ring but I wasn't fazed. I didn't even acknowledge that something was wrong. I zipped up and went back out onto the field. I had worked my whole life for that opportunity and wasn't going to jeopardize it. I couldn't tell the trainer because if I got pulled from the game, there was a good possibility that I wouldn't get back in. They weren't going to hold my spot and I might never get another chance. That's the harsh reality of professional football. Looking back, it obviously wasn't healthy to keep playing but that's how focused I was at the time. Sometimes, that's what it takes.

The casual viewer probably didn't pay any attention to that preseason game between the Patriots and the Panthers, but it's during those games where you find all the guys like me selling out so they can earn a roster spot. They're fighting for their lives out there. Everyone plays with an insane sense of urgency because so many jobs are on the line with final cuts right around the corner.

I had a great game and was all over the place. I finished with a sack and three hurries. There was one play where I smacked quarterback Dameyune Craig right in the mouth. The stadium went crazy. My brother later told me that they showed that play during the highlights on ESPN and he recorded it. I was so pumped after that hit, but as soon as I got to the sideline, Belichick brought me right back down to earth.

"Come on, Marc," he said. "You've got to get the fucking ball out." Coach Belichick always paid extremely close attention to every detail.

After that game, I thought that I had done everything possible to make the team but three days later I was cut. My head was spinning. I was shocked but I was also angry. *What do I have to do? What more do I have to show them?*

At that point, it would be the easiest thing in the world for me to quit but that thought never crossed my mind. I couldn't even consider stopping. I had been through so much. This journey started when I was six years old. I had invested more than a decade of my life in this pursuit. My mother's words still had a profound impact on me, "You just have to hang in there."

That's what I did. I had come far, though nobody but my mother ever thought I'd make it to the NFL. At the time, I could have done plenty of other things with my life that would have been easier, but I wasn't as passionate about anything else. I couldn't change my warrior-like focus when things got tough. There was nothing that could deter me.

Shortly after getting cut from the Patriots, I got a call from Mark Duffner, the defensive coordinator of the Cincinnati Bengals. I had worked out for Coach Duff back at Richmond before the NFL Draft. We got along great, and I must have made a good impression because he wanted to bring me on board.

"Marc, what do you think about coming to play for the Bengals?"

WHAT I LEARNED

Life takes unexpected twists and turns. I never thought that I would travel to Europe, and I definitely arrived with certain expectations in my head, but I couldn't have been more pleasantly surprised by the experience.

CHAPTER 11

THE LIFE OF AN NFL JOURNEYMAN

"Anyone can give up. It's the easiest thing in the world to do. But to hold it together and keep your head up when everyone else would understand if you quit, now that is true strength."

—Chris Bradford, author of *The Way of the Sword*

It took a couple days to clear waivers before I was officially picked up by the Cincinnati Bengals and put on the practice squad.

I shipped my Ford Mustang to Ohio and hopped on a plane for another fresh start. This time around, I knew not to get too comfortable. I checked into a Days Inn Hotel since I had no idea how long I was going to be there. That was a lesson I learned very early in my NFL career. I was in control of my effort. I could make sure that I was well prepared and the best athlete that I could possibly be but there was much more to the league. My stay with the team could end at any time through no fault of my own.

Cincinnati was an interesting city, though there wasn't much going on. It was cold and lonely. I would practice, lift weights, and then hang out at the hotel. That was it. We had a good group of guys on the team but I didn't grow as close to them as I had back in New England. I also didn't have any family in the area so I mostly kept to myself. I was always a movie person. That year, I pretty much saw every movie that came out in the theater. I usually found myself waiting around until the new movies came out on Fridays. If I wasn't watching movies, I was reading everything I could find on training, the body, and psychology.

As an organization, the Bengals were in transition. Head Coach Bruce Coslet had just resigned and they named defensive coordinator Dick LeBeau the interim head coach. Added to this, nobody on the team knew who I was and that was difficult because it's during training camp when players form a bond and start to become a team. I missed it while I went through training with the Patriots. Now, I had to earn the respect of a close-knit group of players. You accomplish that by paying attention to detail and knowing what you need to do. More important, you have to be a good teammate.

I definitely wasn't the first guy to find himself on a new team at the start of a season. It's just the way things go for NFL journeymen. A good journeyman can be inserted anywhere. He needs to fill in and not make mistakes. He may not be a Pro Bowl-caliber player but his asset is his ability to adapt and be productive. I was starting to realize that if I was going to make a career in the NFL, I had to become a reliable player who could be thrust into any situation and thrive.

The Bengals were looking for guys who were tweeners—guys who were not big enough to be defensive ends but a little bit bigger than the average linebacker. Mark Duffner believed in me. He knew I was a lineman at Richmond and thought he could teach me to be a linebacker. I had spent a lot of time with him during the recruiting process before the combine. He was a riot and we got along immediately. I quickly realized why Jim Reid thought the world of him. He was one of the most genuine and authentic coaches I ever had. Even an outsider could see that he cared a great deal about his players. I could tell that he appreciated my hard work.

He used to joke with me and say, "Marc, when are you gonna take out my daughters?"

After four weeks on the practice squad, Coach Duff kept telling me that he was going to get me on the roster as a special teams player. The linebackers were the strong core of the Bengals team. We had a lot of good linebackers so the backups also played special teams because they were the guys who could play anywhere.

Right when things settled down and I started to feel comfortable in my role on the practice squad, it happened: Linebacker Brian Simmons went down with an injury and Adrian Ross was bumped from special teams to linebacker. That opened a spot on special teams. I began to hear rumors that I might be moved to the 53-man roster for an upcoming game in Dallas against the Cowboys.

At the beginning of the week, I finally got a call from Mark Duffner, who confirmed that I was getting bumped up.

"You're gonna play special teams and you better play well," he said. "Give 'em hell."

This was it. This was what I had been waiting for my entire life, and making my professional debut couldn't have happened at a bigger venue than the Cowboys' stadium in front of 62,000 people. I didn't want to get too excited yet. I had been added to the active roster with the Patriots and traveled with the team on the road only to be deactivated before the game. Having had the rug pulled out from under me many times before, I wasn't going to make a big deal out of it. I wasn't going to get too high or too low. I was going to do what I always did.

Practice was a lot more intense that week, and I did it with the intention of starting on all the special team units. Special teams were new to me in the NFL. If you're a dominant player in college, you don't play special teams. It doesn't work that way. But when you get to the NFL from a smaller school and find yourself fighting for a spot, special teams are the way you make the roster. However, making the switch isn't as easy as it seems. Special teams require an entirely different energy level and skill set. The average football play from the line of scrimmage lasts three to four seconds. The average special teams play can last up to 12 seconds.

That week, the coaches paid more attention to me in meetings and on the field. It was their job to mentally prepare me for what I would face that week against the Cowboys. It was my job to be in position and follow through on their instructions. My teammates treated me differently. They all knew how much it meant for me to be activated and they looked out for me more than ever.

After we boarded the flight to Dallas, I watched the rest of the guys to get a feel for their routines. Some studied the game plan package. Others played cards or listened to music. The atmosphere was light but everyone was focused. I studied for a bit and then decided to watch the in-flight movie. The trip went by quickly. We landed and went right to the hotel. With the Patriots, we had to pay extra to get our own room and a lot of guys didn't want to fork over the money; with the Bengals, everyone got their own room.

The night before the game was always well organized. We attended team meetings and the coaches spoke to us. Even some of the vets chimed in. The message was simple: Know your responsibility and do your job.

After a long night of tossing and turning, I headed to breakfast. I always had a light breakfast on game day, usually eggs and oatmeal. I couldn't have too much in my stomach. I wanted to soak in the whole experience and watch all the player rituals and warm-up routines so I got on the early bus to the stadium. As game time approached, the locker room became dead quiet. Each player was in their own headspace as they mentally prepared. It was strange. I was going to run down the field during a regular season game. This was the moment I had been working for my entire life but that's not what I was thinking. I was preparing for a game, just like I had at Richmond and Durfee. I was in my element and I felt like I belonged there.

The Bengals were to kick off and I took my spot on the field. The adrenaline I felt in that moment was like nothing I ever experienced in my entire life. It's difficult to put into words but it was euphoric. I could feel energy start to swell inside me. As soon as the ball was kicked, I sprinted down the field. I think I was the first one down there, which is saying a lot since there were a lot of fast guys on that field.

I thought preseason games were fast but they were nothing compared to the speed of a regular season game. I didn't know human beings could move that fast, never mind human beings wearing helmets and shoulder pads. It involved completely new gear, and I felt panicked about wanting to do everything I could on the field. I felt like a violent, screaming missile running downfield. The collisions were that much more intense.

Unfortunately, the Bengals lost 23-6. But the game was a wild, adrenaline-fueled experience, and in the blink of an eye, it was over.

I accomplished my goal but it felt like I still had more to do. I was reminded of the Greek myth of Sisyphus, who was forced to roll a boulder up a hill for eternity only for it to roll all the way back down when he reached the top. That's kind of how I felt. My goal was never achieved. There was always a new one. Now I wanted to get on the field as a linebacker and I was back at the bottom of the hill all over again.

Looking at the talent before me was humbling. The reality of my situation began to sink in and that led me to question myself. I knew that I wasn't as good as Takeo Spikes. I just wasn't. *Is it even possible for me to work my way into the lineup? Am I good enough?* Before I got too down on myself, I looked at all the other linebackers in the league, specifically at the guys who used to be on special teams and got bumped up to linebacker. Many of them got their chance because somebody in front of them went down with an injury. They had to play well to keep their spot but it was an injury that got them on the field. That's how it happens.

I may not have had Pro Bowl talent but I could still play and I knew that I was one injury away from getting my chance. I just needed that one chance. In the meantime, I was on the special teams' roster and that meant that I was out there on the field.

The next game on the schedule was against my former team, the New England Patriots. You can only imagine how good it felt to suit up and play against the team that cut me. I was out for blood, and with my first regular season game already under my belt, I took the field with more confidence. I felt like I had an edge. I didn't feel as overwhelmed as I did the previous week.

On special teams, I was lined up against Lawyer Milloy, who was the highest-paid defensive player in the NFL at the time. On one play, we ran down the field and he tried to tee me up. I got whacked but he hit me at a weird angle so it actually looked like he got the worst of it. That certainly wasn't true. I fell on top of him and he ended up hurting his knee on that play. He smacked me good, but to everyone else, it looked like Marc Megna just laid out Lawyer Milloy.

Later in that game, I found myself going up against Chris Floyd, another one of my close friends from New England. We battled the whole game. Finally, on one play, I just picked him up and slammed him into the ground. What's funny about football is that you want to hurt your friends on the opposing team the most. We went at it all game, but I had nothing but great respect for both Lawyer and Chris. That's what I miss most about football. Two guys can battle on the field and want to kill each other and still walk away with crazy respect for each other. That doesn't happen in an ordinary workplace, where you have people talking behind your back and trying to throw you under the bus.

I had a great game against New England. Things were looking up for me in Cincinnati and then the unthinkable happened. Multiple wide receivers went down for us in one week. That meant the team needed to pick up wide receivers. Who do they get rid of when they need to make room on the roster? They get rid of the last guy they signed. Me. Mark Duffner called me into his office and broke the news to me.

"I don't know what to say. I'm so sorry," he said.

He called me son and was actually crying when he gave me a hug. That doesn't happen in the NFL. "I think you're a great player and I want you here, but there is nothing I can do."

He told me that he wanted me to stay. "If you're still here in a week, we'll pick you back up."

I told my agent but he had other plans.

"Marc, if you get cut, the Patriots will pick you back up," he said.

I wasn't expecting that and I didn't want it. New England was the last place I wanted to go. Ever since I had been picked up by Cincinnati, I grew to hate the Patriots. They may have been my hometown team but they got rid of me. They told me I wasn't good enough and they didn't want me, so I had no desire to play for them again. Plus, I was in the lineup for the Bengals. I was playing. I knew that I would see more action with the Bengals than with the Patriots. I didn't want the Patriots to pick me up and then put me back on the practice squad. Not only is it much more fun to play but you also make a lot more money.

I was cut by the Bengals and, just like my agent said, New England picked me up. Everything happened so fast that I didn't get a chance to call my mother until I was at the airport waiting to fly home. As soon as I told her that I had been cut, she started crying. I had to calm her down.

"No, no, it's okay because I got picked up by the Patriots," I said. "I'm on my way home."

But she kept crying, saying, "This is so stressful. They don't care about anyone."

When I returned to the New England Patriots facility, part of me felt like I had never left. I hadn't been gone that long, but the one major difference this time around was my confidence. I had come a long way since I last wore the Patriots uniform. The first person I bumped into was Robert Kraft.

"Hey Marc, it's good to have you back where you belong," he said.

That meant the world to me because, as much as I hated the Patriots after they cut me, they were my hometown team. It was also good to be acknowledged by someone like Kraft. He was a class act and always genuine. It didn't matter if you were star quarterback Drew Bledsoe or the last guy on the roster, he always made you feel like an essential part of the team.

The second person I saw was fourth-string quarterback Tom Brady, who said, "What's up, Megs?"

Yup, Tom Brady was the fourth-string quarterback. It sounds insane now but everyone used to make fun of him because he was so gangly and long. People don't realize how small Brady looked compared to Bledsoe, who was so much bigger. The two of them couldn't have seemed more different.

When I was back out on the field with the Patriots, the transition was seamless because I knew the system. It turned out that there weren't a lot of guys who knew Bill Belichick's system. I did well for the Pats while I was there the first time, so getting me back was easier for them than trying to teach the system to someone new.

With Belichick, it was a character thing, too. He looked for character in guys because he was so protective of the energy and the culture in his locker room. Remember, that was Belichick's first year with the Patriots. He was laying down the foundation for the dominant franchise you see today. It started with him hammering home the point that there was no room for error. He wanted everyone to do his job and play mistake-free because if you make mistakes, you can't win. It was that simple with him.

On my first day back with the team, Coach Belichick added me to the roster and special teams coach Brad Seely brought me up to speed. Coach Seely was an unbelievable special teams coach, but I had been convinced he hated me when I was with New England the first time around. It turned out that he actually liked me. One of my former teammates told me that Seely had raved to him about me during a plane flight. I felt like a kid in elementary school who built up a scenario in his head about being disliked when that wasn't the case at all. In the end, teams don't cut you because you're terrible. You get cut because the next guy is just a little bit better.

Coach Seely trusted me enough to put me in the lineup on special teams for the very next game.

He told me, "These are your positions on special teams. You're playing."

And that was that.

The previous Sunday I had played for the Bengals against the New England Patriots. I flew home on Wednesday to join the New England Patriots and got ready to play against the Kansas City Chiefs. Coach Seely did a great job bringing me up to speed before the game, but it was quite the whirlwind journey.

Before I had a chance to process everything that happened, I found myself back in a Patriots uniform and standing in the tunnel, ready to run out on the field for Monday Night Football. I was next to Chris Slade, Willie McGinest, and Tedy Bruschi when some fans above us started screaming my name. All the vets looked at me and rolled their eyes. I tried not to laugh. I just put my head down because it wasn't my place to say anything sarcastic, but it was pretty comical.

I needed a laugh because I was terrified before that game. I have anxiety. As if jumping onto a new NFL team in the middle of the season and being asked to play on Monday Night Football after a couple days of practice wasn't hard enough, doing it with anxiety only added to the pressure. I didn't want to fail. I didn't want to embarrass myself out there, which is easy to do on special teams if you whiff on a block. The truth is that I was scared before every single football game I ever played. Sometimes that fear can be crippling but fear is not always a bad thing. It actually helped me. It's like that line from *Rocky V* when Rocky says, "Your best friend is a guy named Frankie Fear. It keeps you sharp and makes you want to survive but you have to learn how to control it. If you can do that, it will make you hot."

I was on the kick return team for the first play of the game against Kansas City. I had to block this blue-collar All-Pro who was having a great year so I just ran down the field like a madman. As soon as I initiated that first collision, the fear was gone. It suddenly felt like I was back and I went on to play a great game.

The coaches had faith in me because the following week in Chicago, Coach Seely had me blocking one of the fastest guys in the league on kickoff return. This guy was a defensive back who ran a 4.3 forty. *Why would Seely do that? I'm probably one of the last guys you want in that position.*

I was tested early. The first play of the Chicago game was kickoff return. If you're a front-line guy on the kickoff return team, you want to take a fast guy deep. That means you want to run all the way to the kick returner and then turn around to block. With a big guy, you want to take him early so he doesn't build up a head of steam and run right over you. No matter who you're matched up against, you're supposed to wait to see the ball kicked before you sprint your ass downfield.

On that first play, I took off a little early and got about five yards in front of my teammate Kevin Faulk when he caught the kickoff. The second I turned around, the DB from Chicago was already a yard or two away from me. I couldn't believe it. He was right in my face. All I could do at that point was turn my body, but I was still able to clip him as he flew by me. Meanwhile, Faulk ran right up my ass for a 40-yard return. It was one of the best returns of the year. On the film, you can see me on my knees with my finger in the air, celebrating. The fans in the stadium who saw me probably had no idea why I was so happy or even realized that I just blocked the fastest guy in the NFL. The guys on the team knew what happened and were smacking me in the helmet for making a good block. In reality, it was actually a lucky block but you take them any way you can get them.

The following week, we traveled to Buffalo to play against quarterback Doug Flutie and the Bills. Buffalo was freezing. Not only was it snowing but the stadium was like a wind tunnel. The defensive players had a dress code and were not allowed to wear long-sleeved shirts. That was the dumbest rule in the world. Before the game, Larry Whigham was out there warming up in a sleeveless shirt. Meanwhile, I couldn't feel my extremities. The whole field was covered in snow. I couldn't see the yard markers so I didn't even know where to line up. It was difficult to stand, let alone perform. Everything slows down in those conditions.

Once the game started, it was fun watching Flutie run around the backfield. Nobody on our defense could get close to the guy. He was doing work and making short, 5- and 10-yard plays. Toward the end of the game, I had to line up across from Ted Washington on the punt team. He was 6'4" and 365 pounds. You could barely see me. I could have had the best technique and hunkered down but it wouldn't have mattered.

Luckily for me, he was so gassed that he looked up and said, "Don't worry bro, I'm not rushing."

When the ball was snapped, he just stood there. That was the best example of a veteran taking off a play and it couldn't have come at a better time for me. That was a blessing.

We defeated Buffalo in overtime and were 5-10 going into our final game of the season at home against the Dolphins on Christmas Eve. We weren't going to the playoffs that year so everyone knew this would be our last game. I was pumped because I got to match up against Larry Izzo and Derrick Rodgers on special teams. Izzo was a working-class kid from Rice who signed with the Dolphins as a free agent. He started making plays and became this special teams' demon. Rodgers was a former All-American linebacker from Arizona State.

When you're playing on the punt return team and going up against an athletic player like Rodgers, you want to maul them so you can save your legs. When I first watched tape on punt return plays, what surprised me was that you were allowed to hold. Coach Seely said that the refs will give you one sin. That meant that I could hold you by your chest and spin you around once but then I had to let you go. So, when I lined up against Rodgers, that's what I tried to do. I don't know who coached him but they must have done hand work all day because when I tried to hold him, he hit me with a karate chop and then started screaming. *Okay, this guy's a pro.* Once he started running down the field, I didn't have a chance. For the rest of the game, I tried to fake at him and then backed off so I could mess with him as he ran down the field. I had never seen a player who was violent off the ball like that.

We came up short that game. Our third-string quarterback was Mike Bishop from Kansas State who had a rocket for an arm. With only a few seconds on the clock, he was given a chance to throw a bomb that could possibly win the game for us, but it turned out to be a duck that got knocked down at the twenty. The season was over.

Once the stadium cleared out, I went up into the stands and sat there, looking out on the field. Except for a few guys cleaning the aisles, I was all alone, and I wasn't even that cold because I was still running on the adrenaline from the game. It was hard to process all that had happened. I had worked my entire life to get to that point. I thought about the hell that I put my body and mind through. All the training in high school, the torturous workouts, and training camps at Richmond. To me, it wasn't just about football.

Of course, I loved the game dearly, but it was more about achieving a lifelong dream in spite of the critics who told me I wasn't strong enough, fast enough, or good enough to be among the best. The only person who believed in me from the start was my mother. She told me that I would play in the NFL one day and there I was. I had just played another game for the New England Patriots. Sitting there in the freezing cold, I was so overwhelmed with emotion that I started crying and laughing at the same time. It was really an unbelievable moment.

That night, I invited my teammates Kerry Taylor and Garrett Johnson to meet me at my grandparents' house for a traditional pasta dinner. I arrived at the house first and my grandparents were there waiting to greet me at the door.

"Don't worry," said my grandpa, "It's not your fault. You can't do anything. The quarterback is terrible."

For some reason, my grandfather hated Bledsoe, yet he couldn't pronounce his name so he always called him "Tutso."

When they arrived, Garrett Johnson and Kerry Taylor looked enormous in my grandparents' tiny house. Their appetites were even bigger. That was the first time I had ever seen anyone eat more than me at that table. They had five plates of pasta, garlic bread, and meatballs. My grandfather, who typically hated having strangers in the house, was thrilled.

My grandfather had a huge heart, but he knew nothing about sports so I was surprised to see how much he enjoyed following the team. He was French and grew up very poor and worked his ass off to make a better life for his family. My grandparents, who were in their seventies, usually didn't even turn on their television, but once I started playing for the Patriots, my grandfather recorded all of the games on the local radio station. He had a whole collection. He didn't understand what he was listening to at first but said that every time he heard my name on the radio, he knew that I had done something good.

The more the announcers said my name, the better I was getting in his eyes. That was when I started to realize how much the Patriots move people from New England. When they win, the whole region is happy. When they lose, everyone is pissed off and depressed. Football fans who grew up in New England know that to be true.

After the season, Belichick told me, "I see you coming along."

He credited my improvement to all those extra reps I got while playing in NFL Europe. "I'm gonna send you back," he said.

That sounded great to me because I assumed that I'd be returning to Barcelona with Sean Morey but it didn't quite work out that way. The Barcelona team was basically the farm team for about five or six different NFL teams. Some of the other European teams started to complain because Barcelona was getting too many skilled players. As a result, I was sent to play for the Berlin franchise. *What? Who wants to go to Berlin?* The only reason I wanted to return to Europe was the chance to play for Barcelona. I was known in Barcelona. That's where I was comfortable. I didn't know anybody in Berlin. The city seemed cold compared to Barcelona, which was beautiful and right on the beach, but I didn't have a choice.

I was in the same boat as the previous year and had to bust my ass to make the team. We all knew that our NFL futures were at stake and that put way more pressure on everyone during camp. I had to fight because Berlin was only going to keep three linebackers. Luckily, I ended up earning one of those spots.

My season in Berlin was not as memorable or as fun as the previous season in Barcelona. We started by rotating linebackers but when one of those linebackers got hurt, I ended up playing every snap. I also got to play a lot of defensive end so I pretty much did it all on defense.

We practiced in a facility that was a former Nazi barracks. At times, private security followed us because there were Hitler Youth rallies in the area and it wasn't the safest environment for our African-American players. We spent a lot of time at the hotel watching films. Some people loved the team and took care of us but others didn't take to Americans. Club sandwiches were a favorite item on the hotel menu, but we learned early on that the staff would sometimes push the toothpicks deep into the sandwiches so you couldn't see them when you bit into the sandwich. That happened all the time, and it hurt like hell, so we got in the habit of checking our sandwiches before taking a bite.

The fact that the team didn't do so well also put a damper on the experience. We finished with a 5-5 record, but through an unlikely series of events, we found our way into the World Bowl against Barcelona, the best in the league. They were stacked and clearly the favorites. We got stomped the first time we played Barcelona and everyone expected us to get trounced again. Our coach, Peter Voss, also used to be the assistant for Jack Bicknell in Barcelona so it became a grudge match for those two guys, too.

The game was held in a massive venue in Amsterdam. When we took the field, it felt like we were the Bad News Bears. Once again, Barcelona jumped out to a quick lead. Our wide receiver, and my former teammate at Richmond, Dwaune Jones, made a couple of great catches to bring us back. We pulled ahead and kept the lead to actually win the World Bowl. Nobody could believe it. I have a great picture taken after the game of my consoling my former teammate, Sean Morey, who played for Barcelona.

I returned to Massachusetts and got ready for training camp with the Patriots. Berlin may have been uneventful but I finally felt like I had gained my footing. I had paid my dues and I was ready for the 2001 season. I had second-year player status and my confidence was high. I started to feel it.

We hadn't started training camp yet but I knew that year was going to be different. I knew the system and I knew what I needed to do to survive in the league. Then I got a call from the Patriots' front office asking me to come to the facility for a meeting. *Oh no.* This wasn't unusual. It could have been a meeting about football or something to do with operations, but I also knew that I could be getting cut. You never know. That's why I always tried to stay humble and keep an even keel—not get too cocky or confident. I wasn't so lucky this time. The meeting turned out to be one that I feared it would be—and one that, unfortunately, I was getting used to. I was cut by the Patriots. Again.

The more I thought about it, the angrier I got. Training camp hadn't even started yet. *Why did they send me to Berlin if they were going to release me before training camp?* It didn't make any sense. What made that news so much more difficult to swallow was that I was ready to play. I finally knew what I was doing. This was going to be my moment and it was snatched away.

When I first went through NFL preseason, I knew in my heart that I didn't do enough to let the Jets know that I should be there. I was in a locker room with a bunch of All-Pro linebackers whom I still considered my heroes. I deserved to be cut back then, but this time I felt that I had done enough. I gave it everything and I still came up short. It was the most humbling moment of my football career. When you lay it all on the line and you're told it's not enough, that's hard to take. I felt worthy and they were telling me that I wasn't.

After getting the bad news, I returned to the University of Richmond to workout and wait for a call but nobody was calling this time so I started working as the assistant defensive line coach. I knew most of the players because they were freshmen when I was a senior. I enjoyed my time coaching but I wanted to play.

Finally, the call came! It was from the Arizona Cardinals. Instantly, my spirits were lifted. I packed my bag and headed to the airport. But before I even boarded the plane, I got a call from the Cardinals, "Sorry Marc but we signed another guy." *Really? How is this happening?* Back to Richmond I went.

One week later, I got a call from the Pittsburgh Steelers who said they wanted to sign me. Maybe the situation with Arizona was a blessing in disguise. Things happen for a reason, right?

I went back to the airport and held my breath, dreading another last-minute call, but thankfully, that didn't happen. I boarded the plane incident-free and arrived in Pittsburgh. The next day, the coaching staff put me through a series of drills on the field. They clocked my sprints and watched me workout in the weight room. When you're in that position, the coaches want to see whatever you can do. And when you're running a 40 in the grass with cleats on, it's tough to be your best but I did it all. I benched 225 for reps. Then I went back on the field and did pass drops, which were no picnic either. Seven coaches were evaluating every move I made.

When I finished, they told me, "Congratulations! We're bringing you to camp." *Thank God!* I was so fired up. That was the best news I'd heard in weeks.

I joined the team for a meeting the night before training camp was set to begin. I found myself sitting between Jerome Bettis and Kordell Stewart listening to Coach Bill Cowher talk to the players. I couldn't believe it. The Pittsburgh Steelers rulebook was huge. It looked like the Bible.

Coach Cowher said, "We're not gonna go through the book. I'm gonna tell you the one rule we have here: When you have to decide to do the right thing or the wrong thing, do the right thing. Next question, how do you know what the right thing is? If you have to stop and think if it's right or wrong, chances are that it's wrong, so be a true Pittsburgh Steeler and do the right thing."

They fitted me for my equipment and had me sleep in a strange bunk area away from the rest of the team but I didn't care. It was great. I was back! In the morning, I stopped by the office to sign my contract, and a few of the executives sat me down for a talk. I immediately had a bad feeling.

"Marc, we didn't realize you had third-year status," one of them said.

"Okay, what does that mean?" I asked.

"It means that we can't sign you."

The previous night, the Steelers had signed two defensive backs to extensions. Since third-year players receive a salary higher than first- and second-year players, the math didn't work out. They needed a cheaper player.

That was it. Done. It was back to the University of Richmond to lick my wounds.

No more calls came from the NFL after that.

Getting used to my Bengal stripes.

WHAT I LEARNED

Learn how to be flexible and adapt to your environment. Don't become set in your ways. I had never played special teams before the NFL, but I quickly learned that special teams was where I would make my bones in the league and carve out a career. Excelling on special teams was my way onto the roster and ultimately my way onto the field. If I wasn't open to that, I would not be in the NFL.

CHAPTER 12

MONTREAL

"Love what you have before life teaches you what you've lost."

I coached spring football at Richmond and then stayed on as the assistant defensive line coach for the entire regular season as well. That year, I learned a lot about the psychology of coaching. I also gained insight into the recruiting process and how to deal with players from an entirely different perspective.

It was a great experience but something was clearly missing. I loved to coach, but by the end of the season, I felt defeated. My entire NFL experience was psychologically draining. I was doing my best to show people that I was fine and it was no big deal but it was a big deal and I wasn't fine. I was beginning to think my football career was over and trying to figure out what to do with the rest of my life. I started doing things differently. I was still training but more for myself and to make sure I was healthy. That's when I got the call.

This call didn't come from any NFL team. It came from the head scout of the Toronto Argonauts of the Canadian Football League.

"Marc, we have a great league up here," he said. "I think you still have some football left in you. Would you be interested in playing?"

I loved the idea of playing football. I didn't know the first thing about the CFL but they must have had heard of me because Toronto wasn't the only team interested. While Toronto was trying to set up a time to work me out, I got a call from Jim Popp, general manager of the Montreal Alouettes, saying he had acquired my rights.

"Great, what position would I play?" I asked.

"Defensive end," he said. "You'd be a pass rusher."

The guy was saying everything I wanted to hear. I called up my agent to get a sense of the league. He had nothing but good things to say.

"Dude, you'll love it," he said. "Montreal is one of the best teams in Canada. The city is incredible. You're going to have the experience of a lifetime. You gotta go. And if you play well, you might even be able to get back into the NFL."

That was all I needed to hear. Football was football and I wanted to play, so what did I have to lose? Montreal had negotiated for my rights, but I still had to attend training camp and make the team. My agent assured me that it was the smart move.

Up to that point, I had been training with Jim Rooney, one of the assistant strength coaches at the University of Richmond. He was using The Westside Barbell Training System, which incorporates bands, chains, and boards, and is now a staple for all professional athletes. There are four training days—two upper body days and two lower body days. I hurt my lower back in Cincinnati but I was able to rehab. I did everything Jim told me to do and started to feel like I was the strongest I had ever been heading into training camp in Montreal.

I packed my car and left Richmond, stopping in Fall River to visit my family on the way. The team seemed excited to have me so I figured that I'd be a shoo-in to make the roster, but I arrived at camp and walked into a room with 17 other defensive linemen. *Okay? What's going on?* I started doing the math and figured out that I had to beat ten guys. Then I learned that they were only going to keep two Americans, maybe three. I immediately got on the phone with my agent.

"Mike, why would you send me here?"

"Don't worry, you'll dominate."

"Mike, there are 17 guys here, and I'm the shortest and the smallest in the room," I said. "All of these guys are from big-name schools and have NFL experience."

"They aren't looking for that. They're looking for guys like you."

"Come on, what were you thinking?" I pushed.

"Marc, go to camp and bust your ass. Hustle. Do everything possible," he said. "Get to the ball. Get to the quarterback. Create disruption. Do what you do best. Be a lunatic."

Montreal typically had an excellent team but they hadn't won the Grey Cup since 1977. That was under Coach Marv Levy who went on to coach the Buffalo Bills. They also were coming off a terrible season so they brought in Don Matthews or "The Don," as people called him. He was in the Marine Corps before he started coaching and eventually became the most winning coach in CFL history. In his sixties and unmarried, his girlfriend looked half his age. He was a cool guy who loved the players. I liked him immediately.

Matthews wanted to bring new energy to the team so every position was up for grabs. He also wanted a fast defense. He wanted guys who were defensive backs playing linebacker and linebackers playing defensive line. I felt like I had a leg up because I was in a similar situation at Richmond. While cuts were being made, I just kept flying around the field and tried to have fun. I also made sure I was prepared. I watched more game film than ever. I watched film before practice and after practice. Even at night while everyone else slept, I watched it in an old military bunker that doubled as our team room.

The CFL had some terrific players, but they also give a lot of stuff away in that league. In the NFL, the offensive line looks exactly the same every time so as a defender you never know what's coming. The only real tip-offs you get in the NFL come from a team's patterns of down and distance because teams tend to stick with what works for them. In the CFL, it's not uncommon for an offensive lineman to line up in the backfield. That tipped me off that he'd be pulling before the ball was even snapped. I never told anyone this but knowing the plays before they were coming was what helped me succeed at Richmond. In college, I used to turn my ear to the offensive huddle and listen to the quarterback. I was keyed into what he was saying and I could hear the whole play. I learned quickly that I could do the same thing in the CFL. And I did.

In the first preseason game against the Hamilton Tiger Cats, I played left defensive end. As soon as both offensive linemen set up in the backfield, I knew they were pulling. Right before the ball was snapped, I exploded through the inside knee of the offensive lineman. I created a pile to slow down the running back so linebacker Kevin Johnson could jump over the top and hit the back in the mouth. It was a picture-perfect execution, and it looked like one of the best plays ever executed by a defensive lineman and linebacker. That play alone let everyone on the coaching staff know that I could play. My confidence went through the roof and I knew that I was going to make the team. I continued to do very well with the one-on-one pass rush and, sure enough, I ended up making the roster for the Montreal Alouettes in 2002.

My defensive line coach was Chris Jones. He was a country guy from Tennessee infatuated with football. I've been fortunate that at every level I've always had coaches who would rather die than not be able to coach. I had that again here in Montreal, which suited me well since football was the only thing I cared about at the time, too. Chris was only 5'6" and 160 pounds, but he was a smart guy and one of the hardest working coaches I ever met.

We played a defense called Sting, which was taken from the Desert Swarm defense at the University of Arizona. We'd flood the line and then just mad-house rush until someone broke free. That's how Tedy Bruschi was able to lead the nation in sacks when he played at Arizona. When we did this, the other teams didn't even get off the ball. It was like taking candy from a baby. On the other side, our running back was the late Lawrence Phillips from the University of Nebraska. He had been a first-round pick back in 1996, but legal problems forced him out of the NFL. Still, he was a straight baller. The guy could play. He was 6'2" and 215 pounds and just ran over and around everyone. During our season opener, he must have rushed for three touchdowns and 180 yards, all without anybody laying a hand on him. He looked like a grown man being chased by a bunch of kids.

Our team had a great season. We finished the year 13-5 and won the Grey Cup by beating Edmonton. I was named an Eastern All-Star my first year in the league. It was exciting for us but it was also exciting for the people of Montreal who loved their team. I really had never seen such fanfare. After winning the championship, thousands of people celebrated at a parade in downtown Montreal. When the team went out to eat, we got the royal treatment. And I was only just starting to learn about the city.

One night, my teammate Thomas Haskin pulled me aside.

"I'm going to take you to this place but you can't tell anyone where we're going," he said.

I was all in, and the place he ended up taking me was a legendary Italian supper club called Buonanotte. We pulled up and walked right in, even though there were already 100 people waiting outside. The restaurant served dinner at 7:00 p.m. and then again at 10:00 p.m. Around midnight, they took out all the tables and transformed the restaurant into a giant party scene. All the waitresses were gorgeous, and at the end of the night they would let loose and drink with the customers. It wasn't seedy or shady. It was just this incredible scene where everyone was having a great time.

Thomas said, "I'm going to ask you in an hour what you think."

I didn't need an hour. After about 20 minutes, I had fallen in love with the place. I wanted to figure out a way to move to Montreal permanently. I had no desire to return to the US. That's how good my experience was.

One of my first impressions of that club was that the people were cool. Early in the night, a guy spilled a drink on me. I still had an aggressive mindset those days so I put up my fists and was ready to fight. The reaction made me out to be a small-minded, tough guy. And it was not the smartest move since the guy was huge and most likely would've made it an interesting scrap, but he wasn't looking to fight. Just the opposite.

"Oh, my God, my friend. Let me buy you a drink," he said.

His reaction disarmed me. It took me a long time to realize that not everyone was an aggressive prick like the guys of my childhood. The people in Montreal were friendly and genuine.

I started going to Buonanotte all the time because they had delicious food and attracted great people. I even started dating one of the waitresses. She was a nice girl who graduated from the police academy but also worked there waiting tables.

I became close with Max, who was one of the owners. When I first got to Montreal, Max became my guide to the city. He showed me where to go and also where not to go. When people first arrive in Montreal, they always head to Saint Catherine Street, but that's where the tourists go. Go to Saint Laurent Street if you want to live like a local. Max became like a brother to me. He was known and loved by everyone because he was such a good guy. Years later, he would be in my wedding.

When I first arrived in Montreal, I couldn't wait to get out of there but once I got to experience the city and the culture, I never wanted to leave. It was the coolest city I had been to by far. I found a great condo. I had great friends. Everywhere the team went, people treated us well. The team was winning. I was an All-Star, and I loved playing with my teammates and coaches. I felt so blessed and fortunate to be able to have so much fun doing what I loved. When I started my third season in Montreal in 2005, it felt like I was on the top of the world. During our game against Winnipeg, I looked up to the sky and started to think that I needed a new challenge. Things had become routine—eating, training and practice—that I felt ready for a change up. I didn't know it at the time but I was about to be challenged as I had never been before. Be careful what you wish for.

The game started and I went absolutely crazy. I immediately got a sack and was thrilled. The next series, I was covering a punt when the returner cut outside of me. My teammate, Khari Samuel, got clipped in the back. I saw him coming so I jumped but his helmet went right through my knee. I folded and fell flat on my back. At first, I couldn't feel anything. I knew that something was wrong. I didn't know what, but I knew it was serious. My knee swelled and started to feel like Silly Putty. The two trainers on the sidelines gave each other a look that confirmed my suspicions. Later, I heard the trainers tell Don Matthews that I was done for the year with a torn ACL. I was devastated.

I had always been scared of going under during surgery, so I got an epidural and watched my own knee surgery. It was weird seeing the doctors poke around with instruments inside my leg. The ligaments looked like torn paper towels. I didn't know anything about medicine but I knew that it didn't look right. The doctor walked me through the operation, explained what he was doing, graphed in the new ligament, sewed me up, and it was done. Just like that.

I had been paranoid about drugs of any kind after what happened to my father, so I refused to take any pain pills. Not even Advil. That is not something I suggest and if I had it to do over again, I would definitely take the pain medication because it helps keep the swelling down. You need your body to relax and heal. I didn't understand that back then. The doctors had to numb me for surgery, but when that wore off, the pain hit me like a ton of bricks. I was home all alone in my condo trying to recover and I was in tears because it hurt so much. One night, I actually passed out from the pain and woke up the next morning. I spent the majority of those first couple of days in bed with my foot elevated. When I started to feel better, I tried to get up on my crutches. All the blood rushed to my knee and the pain came flooding back.

I always had an explosive first step off the ball. That was my advantage, and I didn't want to lose that so I was anxious to start rehab. The first couple of days were brutal. Anyone who has undergone knee surgery knows how hard it is to get back that range of motion. Lying on my stomach and trying to touch my heel to my butt almost brought me to tears. In spite of the pain, I became a lunatic with my rehab. If it were suggested I do a particular drill once, I'd do it two or three times. I read up on everything related to my recovery. I took vitamins. I even hired someone who conducted sound therapy to heal the injury. She literally came to my condo and played sounds for an hour on huge speakers.

Still, two weeks after surgery, I wasn't getting better. The doctor was trying to tell me that the pain was normal, but I knew something was wrong. He drained my knee and immediately saw that it was infected. They admitted me to the hospital that night and flushed out my knee. I watched the nurse put two yards of gauze into my knee to suck up the pus. I underwent a second knee surgery and had to spend three long and lonely weeks in the hospital. It was the first time that I ever had an injury that kept me off the field, so I was in uncharted territory.

My neighbor, Mary Baxter, came to visit. She was a nosy woman in her sixties who treated me like her adopted son and used to leave trays of brownies and banana bread at my door. Max came to visit me in the hospital every day, too. I was always starving, so he had the Italian restaurant make a pizza and paid a taxi driver to drop it off at the hospital.

All I wanted to do was get back to training. I wanted to be ready for camp in eight months. I screamed at the doctor. Luckily, he was patient with me.

"Marc, you could lose your leg," he said. "Some things in life are more important than football."

I saw the look on the face of the nurse in the room and I knew he was being serious. That hit home. It was all an incredibly humbling experience. This time, they inserted a PICC line, which was basically an IV that ran directly into my heart to help me fight the infection. I had to carry that thing around with me for four months. When I tried to drive back to Fall River for Thanksgiving, I got stopped at the border and was questioned for three hours because the PICC line, which is like a catheter tube, set the machines off.

Surgery is trauma and nobody can force the body to heal. I always went too hard and that's one of the things that hurt me in the long run. I wanted to be the tough guy but that's not how you win. You have to be smart. I have no doubt that this attitude hindered my recovery and it could have possibly contributed to the torn meniscus I suffered almost ten years later. What I should have done was work on one layer of strength at a time to build a strong foundation. Immediately after surgery, it's all about getting the range of motion back in your knee. Then you have to work on strength and that's when everyone struggles. I had absolutely no understanding of body mechanics back then. I just jumped right in and I started squatting and doing extensions without realizing how many steps I had skipped.

When you suffer an ACL injury, you're supposed to take a year off, but I returned to training camp with Montreal eight months later. I may have been back but I wasn't ready. I hobbled through camp. I made the team and I was a starter, but I wasn't blowing anyone away with my play on the field. It wasn't until about halfway through the season that I started to feel like my old self again. In our game against Calgary, I got two sacks in the first half. In the third quarter, I was pass rushing and I beat this huge offensive lineman. I thought I was about to get my third sack, but offensive linemen who have been beaten peel back and come at you from behind. So, this lineman peeled back and caught up after I made contact with the quarterback. He got his helmet on me and drove me right into the ground. He bounced on top of me. I heard my back pop! It was such a strange feeling. At first, it felt like my back was on fire, but I could still move. I played the rest of the game.

That night, I went home and laid on the couch to watch the replay on ESPN. When I woke up in the morning, I had come down from the adrenaline rush of the game and I couldn't move my legs. At the hospital, I learned that I had ruptured three discs.

I was out of commission again, and I didn't even know if I would be ready to play the following season. I just wanted to make sure I could walk. To add insult to injury, Montreal decided to cut ties with me. I found out later that what they did was against the rules. The team wasn't allowed to cut me because of an injury but they did anyway. The player's association stepped in and helped to get me a settlement for the money I was owed on my contract, but from that point forward, I was completely on my own.

I didn't have the support of the team or access to their trainers and doctors. That made things difficult because I wasn't recovering properly. I couldn't stand correctly. One hip was higher than the other. I could barely move. It hurt to walk. I couldn't stand up or bend over without the assistance of a crutch. My feet were slow and I walked gingerly. I had no stability. The pain was indescribable.

I went to a doctor who said, "If you were my son, I'd tell you not to play football again. Walking is more important."

Before I even thought about football, I knew that I needed to get healthy and improve my quality of life. I went deep down the rabbit hole of educating myself on my rehab. *Okay, how am I going to do this now?* It started with light movement in the pool and doing a range of motion exercises with my lower body and hips. I did any sort of cardio that my back could tolerate. I worked on only bodyweight activities in the gym with lots of stretching and yoga. I did everything possible to heal myself. I got massages, and I even brought back the sound therapist. I also was incredibly careful about what I ate because most players pack on weight once they stop playing.

At the start of 2006, harsh reality began to sink in: My football career was over. Only a few months earlier, I was on top of the world. I was an All-Star player who was celebrated by my organization and the city. I was having the best time of my life. If the knee injury cut me down to size, then the back injury knocked me out cold. My career had been in jeopardy before but this was different. This wasn't about effort or pushing myself. This was about my body and not being physically able to perform.

I was all alone, and it was starting to look like everything I spent years working toward was over. That was hard for me to digest. I was in completely uncharted territory. What do I do now? I thought. What *can* I do now?

First Sack as an Alouette

WHAT I LEARNED

Nobody can play football forever. Whether you're an athlete or not, change is inevitable, so you don't want to put all of your eggs in one basket. Plan for your future and consider contingency plans for when things go wrong. No matter how great you may feel at one moment in time, it can all be taken away in a second.

CHAPTER 13

LIFE AFTER FOOTBALL

"The death of your ego will be the beginning of your real life."

While I rehabbed my back during the day, I decided to pursue something at night that I always wanted to do—acting. I liked to watch movies so I figured that acting would be a natural fit. All I had to do was memorize lines, right? I enrolled in classes taught by Jacqueline McClintock. We learned about the Meisner technique, and I enjoyed the classes tremendously, but I quickly learned that there was much more to acting than I initially realized.

Jacqueline became a close friend of mine and I followed her to Toronto when she moved there to teach. I performed a scene from a play called *The Wool Gatherer* that helped me earn a scholarship to attend the Mallorca Film Academy in Spain where I had the unique opportunity to work with other international student actors.

When I returned to Montreal, my work visa was about to expire. I had one to play football but I couldn't get a visa to do anything else and they wouldn't let an American take a paying job away from a Canadian citizen. I had to find a new place to live.

In the past, I had been to Miami to train in the off season. It was a great city. I liked the people and I loved the energy so it seemed like a good fit for the time being. When I arrived in South Beach in June 2007, I rented an apartment that was way too expensive. I quickly had to find a new place to live that was more affordable.

Money was becoming a problem and I questioned whether I would be able to live in Miami and have a long-term career. I needed a job and a friend offered me a position selling advertising space on a local television show. The show highlighted the top restaurants, nightclubs, and bars in the area. I found myself wearing a new type of uniform—a suit. I hated wearing that thing. It was restricting and uncomfortable.

Even more uncomfortable than the suit was the job itself. I knew something was off. I quickly realized that the show was a scam, a feeble attempt by the creator to establish herself as a reputable TV personality. I was embarrassed. I didn't like the sales pitch or the energy that surrounded the business. I knew in the pit of my stomach that the job was not for me so I quit. I had never quit anything in my life. From a very young age, it had been drilled into my head that quitting was never an option. That's what made it so hard to do, but I knew that I had to get myself out of a bad situation.

It may have been a necessary step but it also meant I was back at square one. I needed a job. I needed to figure out what I wanted to do with my life and I needed to do it fast because I didn't have much money. It didn't help that I was in an unfamiliar city.

As difficult as that time was, I still kept doing the only thing that I knew how to do and that was to train like a professional athlete. Working out was what I loved and it will always be a part of who I am. I had to simulate practice to make it feel like I was doing something worthwhile. I would wake up before the sun rose and start my day off with a five-mile run on the beach. I'd then hit the Flamingo Park pool for a few hundred laps and some intervals. After a quick lunch, I'd go to the gym and then maybe take a kickboxing or boxing class at night. I was trying to recreate the training process.

I worked out at several facilities in Miami. There was Crunch, David Barton, and The Grid Iron Club, but Equinox became my favorite. It was nothing like the gyms where I worked out when I was a kid. In those dungeons back home, I was lucky to find a pair of matching dumbbells. In Miami, the gyms were clean with new equipment.

I weighed about 240 pounds when I arrived in Miami, but after about six months of my grueling exercise routine I was down to 190. I felt like Christian Bale in *The Machinist.* I didn't realize it at the time but I was torturing my body with those workouts. Exercising makes my mind pop. That's when I do most of my thinking and that's when I find solutions to the problems bothering me at any given time. At that point, the problem was simple: I wasn't working and I still had no idea what I was going to do with my life.

When you're a pro football player and you learn that your career is over, you usually go into coaching or become an analyst. Football is all you know. You've invested a lot of time and energy in your craft, so it's a wise move to stay in the game because you can build on that experience and evolve. I could have worked toward that. I had coached at Richmond and I loved the time I spent there on the sidelines but it wasn't for me. I saw the life coaches lived. Those guys never got to spend time with their families. More important, it wasn't something I was passionate about. I knew the game but I didn't have the burning desire to be a football coach and that's something you need if you're going to put in that kind of time. If you don't love it, it's a recipe for disaster.

The funny thing was that I wasn't that passionate about football anymore. People invited me to see the Patriots play when they were in town. They tried to get me to go out to bars or over to their houses to watch the games but I didn't even want to do that. I made up excuses. It's not that it was hard to watch but I had lost interest. I invested 20 years of my life into the game. I watched film two or three hours every day. Add to that all the countless hours of practicing, running, lifting, and being utterly obsessed with football and I finally had had enough. In a way, it reaffirmed what I had come to suspect: What I really loved was the process and the training. That was my fuel.

What I'd been looking for since I arrived in Miami was right under my nose the entire time. A conversation with Anwar Stewart, my good friend and former Montreal teammate, led me to connect the dots.

He knew my frustration and told me, "Man, you should be training people."

"What do you mean?" I asked.

So much heart in this pic. My mom and grandmother taught me so much about life.

Max was one of my closest friends in Montreal, and was a groomsman in my wedding.

Arnold was a huge influence on my life. We share the same birthday, July 30th.

"You know what you're doing, people listen to you, and you love it," he said. "Plus, you could probably make a lot of money."

I put myself on a very specific training program with all the knowledge I had picked up along the way from various strength coaches throughout college and the NFL. Over time, I had started to understand what strength and conditioning was all about. I had healed my back with the Westside Barbell Program. Back in Montreal, guys would come up to me in the weight room and say, "What are we doing today?" They looked to me for guidance and I put some of them through off-season programs.

What Anwar said made sense. I studied the body and recovery during my injuries and I continued to study after I arrived in Miami. Training other people seemed like a natural fit. Only a few days after that call, I was approached by Yvonne Castaneda who headed the personal training department at Equinox. She asked if I wanted to start working as a trainer.

"I do, but I don't have any experience or certification," I said.

"We can help you get certified."

I was going to Equinox all the time and she took notice. She also liked my NFL background so it seemed like a natural fit. Two people in a matter of days came to the same conclusion. It was fate. I have no idea why I'd never thought of it before.

Overnight, I went from being jobless to getting a job doing the one thing I had always been the most passionate about. Getting started wasn't easy, but I finally had an opportunity and I wasn't going to let it pass me by. Not only did I have to get certified but I had to start out as a floor trainer. They gave me a blue shirt and I became a glorified maintenance worker. I had to rack dumbbells and pick up dirty towels.

I had the opportunity to talk to members and stir up business but the job was not glamorous. In fact, I was downright disrespected by some of the other employees.

One time, a manager threw me a towel and said, "Someone spilled something on the floor. I need you to clean it up."

Technically, it was my job, but the smug look on his face said it all. He was trying to humiliate me. Not even a year earlier, I was playing pro football in front of thousands of people and now I was scrubbing a floor. I was mad at first and thinking about creative ways to kill the guy but I took a different approach. Instead, I was going to make that floor shine.

On my hands and knees, I scrubbed that floor hard. The manager looked at me like I was crazy. It didn't stop there. I went and got some floor cleaner to go the extra mile. That pissed him off, but he got the message that I was going to do whatever he asked me to do. I didn't care what the task was; I gave it everything I had.

While working the floor for a couple months, I studied and passed my Certified Strength and Conditioning Specialist exam. But I still knew nothing. Just because you like to workout and can kill it in the gym doesn't mean that you're a personal trainer. I had a long way to go, but I was putting in the work and going the extra mile.

My attention to detail helped me find my first client. Her name was Audrey Bennati and she walked up to me and said, "I want to train with you." I didn't find out until later that she approached me after seeing me stop in the middle of the gym to pick a piece of lint up off the floor.

"You pay attention to detail," she said.

I brought everything I needed to one area and trained Audrey in the middle of the floor at Equinox where everybody could see. She already was a fitness freak in phenomenal shape so I had to challenge her. It was my first shot at session programming for a client. I put hours of thought into her program. We did dynamic movements and strength movements. I tried to make sure I covered all my bases and gave her the best session possible. She loved the training. We did strength work, mobility work, and lots of movement-based training.

I tried to attract as much attention as possible, and it worked. I quickly took on more clients. I would even train people for free and tell them not to pay me unless they felt they were getting something out of it. I wanted to get them results and improve their quality of life.

I told them, "Instead of paying me, go out and tell a few people so I can expand my client roster."

I still felt a lot of pressure. Training paying clients was much different than the off-season training programs I ran teammates through in Montreal. I was being handed my own business and it was mine to lose. I had the life and safety of a client in my hands. They were paying serious money for my knowledge and I was expected to give them results.

I studied and tried to learn all I could but all that did was remind me of how much I didn't know. I took an RTS (Resistance Training Specialist) program that focused on biomechanics and how force is applied to the body during training. It was taught by Peter Chiasson and Eric Seifert. After the first half of the day, I felt completely overwhelmed. Pete saw me slumped in the corner with a defeated look on my face.

"What's wrong, buddy? Are you okay?" he asked.

"I can't do this for a living," I said. "I know nothing."

He laughed. "It takes a lot of time to be great, but the fact that you think you need to be better is everything."

At that moment, I decided that I wanted to be a great trainer. I committed myself to the process of learning daily. I gave up the majority of my free time and most of my recreational activities. I was in class when everyone else was at pool parties or relaxing with friends. I spent countless hours working through the night. There were times when I questioned my priorities. It was challenging and the process is still difficult for me. It takes more than reading magazines and watching YouTube videos. I had to learn how the body moved. I had to learn how to be safe. I had to learn the science. I also had to make mistakes so I could learn from those mistakes.

After every pay period, the managers at Equinox would put up a giant sheet of paper with the top five trainers who accumulated the most sessions during that period. I wasn't even on that list at first, but I told myself that I would soon be on the top of it.

I kept busting my ass, but the money wasn't coming in fast enough. I never thought of myself as being down-and-out. My mind didn't work like that. I always tried to take the bull by the horns and make things happen. I had good friends who helped me out when I needed it, but I was down to my last $200 and my situation was looking dire.

One afternoon, I had just finished a track workout at Flamingo Park and was sitting in my beat-up truck, dripping sweat and feeling completely wiped out when my phone rang. The last thing I wanted to do was talk but something compelled me to pick up. I heard a woman with a Midwestern accent on the other end.

"Is this Marc Megna?" she asked.

"Yes, ma'am."

"Golly gee, I've been trying to find you for three years."

"Can I ask what this is regarding?"

"My name is Julie from the Cincinnati Bengals front office," she said. "I have a check for you. We just haven't been able to track you down."

"Can I ask how much the check is for?" I asked, thinking it was going to be fifty bucks.

"Absolutely. It's for $15,000."

I couldn't believe it. As soon as I got off the phone, I screamed, "I'm back in the game!"

That money gave me the breathing room I needed to keep myself afloat while I built my business. And it took off. When I first started working at Equinox, I was ranked 1,398 out of 1,400 trainers in the company when it came to production and the number of sessions performed. Five pay periods later, I was 13.

I started to train everyone I could and I quickly built up a great roster of clients who couldn't have been more different from one other. I had a couple of doctors, a pharmacist, a teenage boy, and an All-Star softball player. One of the doctors was always on call, so he didn't know if he could make his late session until the last minute. There was a 24-hour cancellation policy at Equinox but I told him that I didn't care.

"I'll be here," I said. "Show up if you can make it."

After my second year at Equinox, a woman asked if I could train her husband at their house because he wasn't a member.

"Yeah, I can do that," I said.

When you're a trainer and you leave a gym, it can come back to bite you, especially in Miami Beach. I had to be really smart when it came to my schedule and travel time. I would finish a session at Equinox at 11:00 a.m. and run out of the gym to make it in 15 minutes to a private session. I'd be there for an hour and return to Equinox for my 12:30 p.m. gym client.

My schedule was slammed and I didn't have a minute to myself, but I always made it a rule to treat my clients like family. Caring for clients wasn't a trick. You actually had to care. Once a client saw that you cared, you had that client for life. It sounds cliché but I never got into training for the money. I did it because I loved the people with whom I worked.

When I started, I trained everyone I could and there were a lot of people whom I didn't like being around. After a few years, I could cut those people loose and only keep the clients I wanted, the ones who were a positive influence with good energy. I was investing in them and they were investing in me. I don't know if I was any good or not. Some people said I was, but I'll let them say that. I made sure to put my time and effort into their programming and my continuing education. If I did that, I knew the money would come. I started off training people for free. Then I was charging $30 an hour. These days, it's a lot more and I believe it's worth every penny.

It took me a long time and a lot of hard work to get to that point. That's why it kills me when I hear trainers who have only been at it for six months say, "It's hard for me to pick up clients. This isn't working out."

"Dude, you've been doing this for six months. What do you expect?" I want to say. "You've put in no time and you're already giving up. Are you training people for free to get them interested? Are you waking up early? Are you staying late?"

Trainers come and go in Miami. People want a big name and a huge following, but they don't understand the first thing about the craft. The ones who try to skip steps will never understand the process. I see a lot of people look for shortcuts to greatness or focus more on becoming online personalities than on the quality of their work. It takes sacrifice and focus. It also takes time, effort, and patience. There are no shortcuts.

This is what experience taught me: Value micro-progressions and trust the process. There are very few people in life willing to put in the time, effort, and commitment to achieving what they really want. Gather a lifetime of knowledge and never think you've arrived. Get rich slow and appreciate it. If you have opportunity and money handed to you, you're never going to appreciate it.

The benefit of hard work and slowly earning your success is that it helps you understand what it takes to build something. It also gives you the tools needed to overcome adversity. No matter who you are or what you do, there will always be challenges waiting around every corner. That's what happened to me when I was starting to hit my stride as a trainer at Equinox. I was gaining confidence in what I was doing and my business was taking off. As if on cue, that's when fate swooped in to keep me in check.

Given my schedule, I was on my feet all day. I started to feel pain in my right foot so I went for an MRI. The doctor, who happened to be the foot doctor for the Miami Heat, told me that I had cracked a bone. He thought it was an injury that occurred during my last season of football and only got worse after being on my feet all day. My body wasn't used to standing for 12-15 hours a day. It wasn't serious. I'd be fine, but he wanted me to stay off my feet for a few weeks. That wasn't possible. I needed to work, so I ended up wearing an air cast for six months. Luckily, I didn't miss a beat.

My reputation as a trainer was starting to grow. People reached out to me online and that led to more opportunities. One of those people was Andrew Garven, a former assistant for the Montreal Alouettes. He was a great guy and smart as a whip, but the players would screw with him and treat him like shit because he was the low man on the totem pole. He was like an assistant to an assistant. He worked hard for us and nobody appreciated him, which I thought was bullshit. The guy basically missed out on his entire twenties because he was breaking down video for us. He was always at the facility before everyone else arrived and stayed there after everyone left. He did all this while going to school. He instantly had my respect and we became friends.

As my personal training business took off in 2009, Andrew hit me up on Facebook. What's funny is that the previous night I had seriously considered deleting my account. I thought social media was superficial but someone convinced me to leave it up. The very next day, I received a message from Andrew, who told me he was working for a supplement company called MuscleTech. They were looking for a sponsored athlete to become a brand ambassador.

"We need someone who is an everyday guy," he said. "Someone between a bodybuilder and a runner. Would you be interested?"

I always thought it would be cool to work for one of those companies but I never had a way in.

"What do I have to do?" I asked.

"Well, nothing right now," he said. "I'll send you our products. If you like them, you can become one of our sponsored athletes and we pay you for it."

"Really? How much do I get?"

"I'll send you over a contract."

I'm not going to say exactly how much it was but my jaw dropped when I saw the figures. I was on board immediately because it was an unbelievable amount of additional income. I hadn't even done anything yet. It felt like free money.

They told me to diet and do what I had to do to get strong and muscular for a photo shoot in two months. I thought I'd get lean by doing what I usually did: Swim, run, and bike. Little did I know that's not the best way to get ripped for a photo shoot. I was a lean-looking guy to begin with but my muscles weren't popping out. I got to the photo shoot and took off my shirt. The photographer started snapping pictures. When he went over to the computer to look at the shots with the crew, I could tell that they weren't too happy. Andrew pulled me aside.

"What've you been doing?" he asked.

"Mostly running, biking, and swimming."

"No, man. You gotta pump weights, pump weights, pump weights."

Okay. I could do that, but I needed help with the diet. I had never done anything like that before. I've always eaten clean, but this was a much different task. He gave me the number of a woman named Adele Friedman, a nutrition and aesthetics guru who would become a lifelong friend. She had done thousands of body transformations and put me on a crazy diet plan. I took vitamin supplements with fish oil, krill oil, and even apple cider vinegar. I ate fish and steak and then no fish and just steak. I ate carbs and then no carbs. It was intense, but a few months later, I went back to the photo shoot and I was in the best shape of my life. I was absolutely shredded.

That shoot led to more work. I eventually got into *Men's Health* and *Men's Fitness*. I then landed the cover of a magazine called *Natural Muscle* and another called *Maximum Fitness*. I started to write more content for MuscleTech and *Bodybuilding.com*. I enjoyed it, even though I didn't really know what I was doing at first.

One day, as I was training my client Rich, he asked, "Why aren't you on the cover of more magazines?"

"Well, I'm not that big of a name in the industry."

"You should call MuscleTech and tell them that you want to be on the cover."

"Rich, it doesn't really work like that," I said.

"You should try it anyway."

Right after the session, I called up my PR contact at MuscleTech and asked him about the possibility of getting on a cover. He made a few calls and a week later I learned that I was being considered for the cover of *Muscle & Fitness.*

Muscle & Fitness was the biggest magazine in the industry at the time and landing a cover was like reaching the top of my profession. It was huge news!

"Absolutely," I agreed. "When?"

"Ten days."

Wait, what? Ten days? How am I going to get ready for the biggest photo shoot of my life in ten days? I immediately put down the food in my hand. I went to the gym and crushed it. I started eating perfectly so I was as ready as I could be when it was time to go.

The company flew me out to New York and arranged a car to take me to their office in New Jersey. While I was waiting, a guy with a bald head and a red beard showed up.

"Hey, are you Marc Megna?" he asked.

"Yes, I am."

"I'm going to shoot you for *Muscle & Fitness* today. If we get some good shots, hopefully you'll end up on the cover."

"Great. You must do this all the time," I said.

"Nope. I've never done this before."

I started to panic.

"You've never shot a cover before?"

"No, I've never shot a cover for *Muscle & Fitness* before," he said. "I shot a guy for the cover of another magazine last week."

Come to find out, the guy he was talking about was Bill Clinton and the magazine was *Time*. This guy was a super pro.

The shoot went great and I wound up on the cover of the January 2012 issue. Arnold Schwarzenegger had been on the cover the previous month so it completely blew me away. January was the month when everyone tried to get into shape. It was also the month when everyone traveled so people picked it up at the airport, making the issue popular. I may not have gotten paid anything for the magazine cover but it led to more people reaching out to me.

I wrote more articles and tried to get on more websites as a way to expand my brand. And it all started because I made that call to MuscleTech. In other words, I asked. The people who get what they want are the ones who ask for it. If you don't ask, you'll never know.

A short time later, MuscleTech came to me with an idea to create a series called "Workout Wednesday," where they'd post my workouts online. Not long after it went up, I saw there were 1,000 comments so I assumed that people liked it. I was excited as I sat down to read them. That was the worst idea ever. About 990 comments ripped me to shreds: "This guy's a joke." "He has no legs." "Where are his shoulders?" "Why doesn't he train abs?" They were tearing into my soul, but it taught me a valuable lesson about being in the public eye and posting content on social media. It's difficult to put yourself out there. With more exposure comes more criticism, and if you're going to throw your hat in the ring, you have to be able to take the good with the bad.

In spite of the criticism, I have to admit that it felt great to see myself on the cover of magazines, but that was never the primary goal. I never did any of it for the notoriety but the notoriety allowed me to reach more people. The real goal was trying to pass on the knowledge about how to lead a healthy lifestyle through training and nutrition.

Through it all, I kept training clients at Equinox and my new exposure allowed me to attract some high-profile athletes as clients. I received a call from Alex Rodriguez and began training him. I loved training all types of clients but I found myself relating to athletes because of my own life experience. I told this to a friend named Danny Martoe, whom I met at Equinox. He was a friendly guy, also from the East Coast and we got along great. He also was a sports agent who worked for Drew Rosenhaus so he was plugged into the athletic community.

"There's only one place to go," he said. "You have to work at Bommarito Performance because Pete is the best."

"Okay then," I said. "Can you get me a sit-down with Pete?"

Pete Bommarito was the go-to guy when it came to training pro athletes. He got college players ready for the combine, and he worked with all types of NFL and MLB players in the off season. There was nobody in the private sector who did what Pete did. He loved his job and he had a reputation for being the best in the industry because he would go above and beyond to make sure his clients and athletes were doing well.

Danny and I met with Pete at a restaurant in Miami. Pete walked in lugging three huge bags of equipment because he didn't want to leave his stuff in the car. I thought that was hilarious. He interviewed and hired me on the spot and I began working for him the next week.

The only problem was that I couldn't give up my job at Equinox. I was making a lot of money and I had no idea how much I would be able to make with Pete so I had to find a way to make it work. I woke up at 4:00 a.m. to run on the beach and train myself. I drove to Equinox at 5:15 a.m. to train clients until about 10:00 a.m. I drove over to Bommarito Performance to work from 10:30 a.m. to 5:30 p.m. and then headed back to Equinox to train clients until 8:30 p.m. I'd go home at night, prep my food for the next day, and try to go to bed early.

Throw in photo sessions here and there and that was my routine for more than two years. It was a grind but it was a hell of an experience. I made sure to keep my mouth shut and my head down, and I tried to learn as much as I possibly could.

At Bommarito, I trained college football players getting ready for the combine and put current NFL players through off-season workouts. I worked with athletes like Wes Welker, Antonio Brown, and Brandon Spikes. We trained Rob Gronkowski for the combine. He got so excited, he was like a little kid, but he came in right after hurting his back. He was a wreck and could barely walk. Some people said that he was done and would never be able to play in the NFL because of his injury. We put him on a machine called the AlterG, which was a treadmill with a pair of pants you stepped into, so it worked sort of like a gravity machine. You program the percentage of body weight carried by your legs when you run. Five weeks later, Gronk ran a 4.6 forty while weighing 255 pounds, which was incredible.

We had another guy come in to train who had a lot of hype around him because he had only been playing organized football for a few years. He was 6'4" and 280 pounds with tremendous athleticism. His name was Jason Pierre-Paul. We put him through the regular exercises. He could only bench 225 five times, so he wasn't strong but he was a ridiculously smooth athlete who could run and move like nobody we had ever seen. How many people that size can do 13 backflips in a row? Being able to work closely with athletes of that caliber and learn programming for specific purposes gave me valuable insight into the training process. Bommarito was a crash course in corrective exercises, bio-mechanics, and the best approaches for specific medical conditions.

It felt like I had found my niche. I learned from so many incredible people along the way and that allowed me to do what I loved. When you're building something, it's easy to get wrapped up in the process, but life has a way of reminding us what's really important. I didn't realize it at the time, and I could never have anticipated it, but I was about to experience the most heartbreaking challenge of my life.

WHAT I LEARNED

When one door closes, another door opens. I was lost after football, but I slowly found myself doing something else that I loved. Remember what it is that makes you unique and start from there when forging a new path. If you have developed good work habits and put in constant effort, that will translate to the next phase of your life so you're never completely starting over.

CHAPTER 14

MOVING ON

"I'm coming for everything they said I couldn't have."

—Amiyah Scott

I had just gotten out of a relationship when my friends set me up with Melanie Tillbrook. She was a single, working model who had represented a supplement company, so we had something in common. Friends who knew us thought we'd hit it off. The plan was for a group of us to all go out together on St. Patrick's Day, but she never showed up. I was disappointed, but I put it out of my mind for the time being.

The following week, I attended a charity event. From across the room, I saw a familiar face, a girl I recognized but couldn't quite place. It was driving me crazy. Finally, I put two and two together. It was Melanie. Later in the evening, I pulled her aside when she walked by.

"I'm sorry but is your name Melanie?" I asked.

"Yes, is your name Marc?"

We talked for two hours that night. The first thing I noticed was her positive energy. She was a genuinely happy person and I loved that about her. We had one of those conversations that I didn't want to end. I needed to see her again but I had friends visiting from out of town that weekend so I asked her if she wanted to come along.

"We'll be going out to eat for the next couple nights. How about joining us for dinner on Friday, Saturday, Sunday, and Monday?" Yes, I actually asked her that.

It got a laugh from her, even though that wasn't my intention.

"How about we just start with Friday and see how it goes?" she replied.

On Friday night, we went out as a group to Nobu. Patrick Dempsey from *Grey's Anatomy* was sitting directly behind us. The whole experience was a lot fancier than I was used to. I was out of my element and that only made me more nervous. I don't know if I wanted to get out in front of it but at the start of the evening, I leaned over to Melanie and said, "I want to tell you two things. First, you look beautiful. Second, I don't usually go to fancy restaurants like this that often so don't get used to it."

We held hands that first night and I saw her as a caring, compassionate, humble, light-hearted, and easy-going person. I made a list of all the qualities I wanted in a partner and she had them all. We clicked immediately and had the same beliefs about life, family, and healthy living. I immediately wanted to spend more time with her.

My personal life was changing and so was my business. After working at Bommarito Performance for nearly three years, I found that training athletes was a double-edged sword. I loved the idea behind what we were doing but it was hard to stand back and watch athletes not work hard. Don't get me wrong, there are a lot of hard workers out there and guys whom I loved but there were others who bitched and complained. Those guys wound up being solid players but they were never as special as they could be. Each time I saw that happen, it took a little bit of something from my soul. I would much rather train an older woman who showed up to work hard than some of the pro athletes who just went through the motions. It felt like some of my regular clients just wanted it more.

In other ways, training athletes is actually easier than regular people. Professional athletes are professionals for a reason. Fitness is already a part of their lifestyle. They already have tremendous strength and speed. As a trainer, it's like you're being handed this awesome canvas on which to paint. It's more of a challenge with people who have varying ability and fitness levels.

I wasn't quite sure what my next step should be. I had multiple clients tell me that I should open my own place. The thing that was unique about Bommarito was that they trained everyday people alongside NFL players. It was a pretty cool environment, especially if you were a kid playing high school football or an executive who found yourself in a group with five NFL players. Pete focused his business around athletes, but it got me thinking about opening a gym where you could train like an athlete and also recover like an athlete.

Nobody was doing that sort of thing. There wasn't a good fitness and wellness country club anywhere in Miami. Typically, if a place had a good spa, the gym usually sucked, and if a place had a good gym, the spa sucked. I wanted to take the extensive list of recovery modalities at Bommarito Performance and make it available to the general public. I was thinking about pool work, cold tubs, infrared sauna, the hot whirlpool, and an IV lounge—every medical and recovery component you could imagine.

I wanted to educate people about how to heal their bodies. Not just for their next workout but for them to feel better about their lives. I wanted to train people for longevity. I also wanted something of my own.

It was a great idea but I had absolutely no idea how to make it happen, and I didn't think I was capable of putting something like that together on my own. I mean, I didn't even know how to use the computers at Bommarito Performance. How was I going to build an entire gym from the ground up?

I also felt that I needed to put in more time as a trainer. I wanted to get more experience in the industry before planting my flag at one location. In reality, part of me was scared. I didn't want the responsibility of having ten trainers depending on me. I didn't want the extra stress. But the more I thought about it, the more I realized how lucky I had been to be taught by excellent coaches and trainers who molded me into something I was proud of. I had learned a lot and I had a lot to offer. It would be a disservice not to pay it forward. I couldn't let my own fears and anxieties hold me back.

There is never an optimal time for something like that. You have to take the plunge, and I knew that if I didn't do it then, I would probably never do it. I didn't want to be one of those people who talked about doing something but never acted.

I needed help and a longtime friend, Danny Martoe, started helping me late at night after work to brainstorm and work on a business concept. We were good friends and I had helped him out with training so he agreed to help me in return. Danny had a friend named Chris Paciello, who also was looking to open a fitness club. Chris had several successful nightclubs back in the '90s and he currently had a spa inside the Delano Hotel. He wanted to couple that with a gym. Chris was very health conscious and trained daily, but he didn't know the fitness and wellness industry as a trainer would.

Danny brought us together because he thought we would complement each other and create something special. I needed to get to know Chris. I didn't know anything about him. I wanted to make sure that he was a guy I could trust. It turned out that Danny's instincts were right. Chris and I got along very well. I liked Chris because he was a creative thinker, ambitious, and wasn't afraid to work. I'll never forget when Chris and I were inside of a commercial dumpster in the Anatomy parking lot the night before we opened. We desperately needed it removed. However, we had to make sure no trash was overflowing. Chris and I used our hands and feet to crush the rubbish together. I immediately knew he was a worker.

But even having found a good partner in Chris, this was a big leap for me and I felt apprehensive about taking such a big risk. I was certainly nervous. I turned to my friend, Randy Frankel, for advice. Randy was part owner of the Tampa Bay Rays and owned a long list of businesses. We met at Equinox. Like my first female client, he approached me when he saw me cleaning up the floor.

"Why are you doing that? You're not the owner," he said.

"That really doesn't matter," I said. "I treat the place like it's my own. We all have to do our part. We're a team here."

I think he appreciated that. As I got to know him, he became like an older brother and a mentor to me. He was a genuine and sincere guy with a big heart. I frequently leaned on him for advice. I'm sure there were many days I drove him nuts with all my questions but there were few people in the world I respected more than him. If this gym concept sounded terrible and wasn't going to work, I could trust him to tell me that. We sat down and I told Randy what I wanted to do.

Not only did Randy encourage me to do the deal but he came on board to back the project. We couldn't have done it without him. I'm not sure Randy will ever know how much I appreciated what he did. He believed in me and he saw the possibility for success. It really meant the world to me. We now had three like-minded people on board and we were committed to building a gym that was unique. We were off and running.

Chris found the building. It wasn't an ideal space but it was located in one of the most popular neighborhoods in Miami Beach. It was previously an old funeral home that would require a great deal of work. If we were going to have a chance at success, it would have to be in that area. All three of us came in with ideas for what we each wanted to do. I had learned a lot about equipment over the years from training and working in different facilities so I compiled a detailed list of what we needed. I wanted to make sure we had the things our members liked and not just what I liked. We found great treadmills, bands, benches, and specialty bars. In the end, we respected each other's visions and benefited a great deal from each perspective.

Chris was in charge of construction, a process that took several months. Miami Beach permitting was notoriously slow. While the building was coming together, we still didn't have a name. We subscribed to a service and each of us was sent a long list of possible names. We circled the ones we thought were best but most of them were just awful names: Miami Fusion. Miami Fitness Factory. We didn't like any of them. One day, the person in charge of the construction crew came to us with an idea, saying, "I got a great name for you. Why don't you call it Anatomy?"

All three of us hated the name at first, but the more we thought about it, the more the name grew on us. It wasn't long before we all agreed that we would name the facility Anatomy. We were set to open our doors in December 2014. Chris brought an incredible positive energy to Anatomy that helped us grow from day one.

A brand-new business venture wasn't the only thing going on in 2014. Melanie and I had been together a few years by then and had decided to get married. I planned to propose during a trip to Italy but I ended up backing out. Not because I was having doubts but I didn't like the ring I had picked out. She was special to me. I wanted to make sure that I spoiled her and

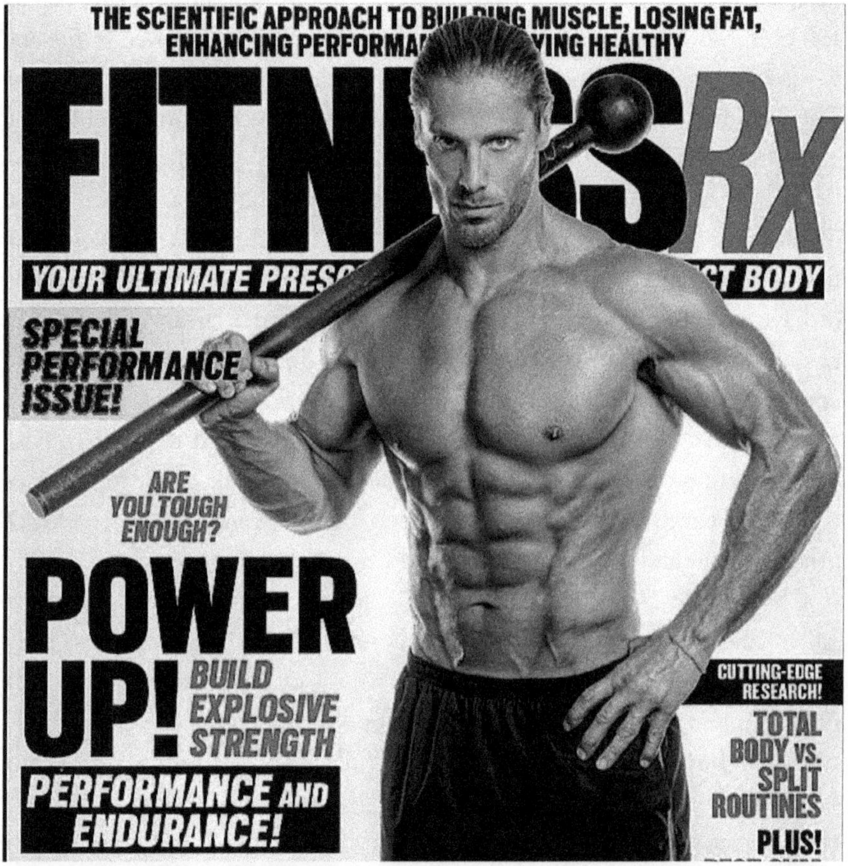

No matter how many times I do this, I still feel awkward getting my picture taken.

Speaking to the students at the University of Richmond.

My brother Mike, my hero.

showed her how much I loved and appreciated her. The best way I knew how to do that at the time was with a ring.

It may sound silly but I felt strong enough to hold off on the proposal. When we got back from Italy, I immediately went ring shopping again and I was able to find one that I liked much better. I proposed on our trip to the Turks and Caicos a few months later and she said yes.

Life was good. I was excited about the future. I couldn't have asked for more, and that's when life smacked me in the mouth again. I had been visiting Boston and was about to board a plane back to Miami when I received a call from my brother.

"I'm not sure how serious it is but I had to take Mom to the hospital because she wasn't feeling well," he said.

They didn't know what was wrong at the time but since he said it wasn't serious, I boarded my flight. When I landed, I learned that the doctors had taken my mom by ambulance to a Boston hospital. She had suffered a cerebral amyloid angiopathy, also known as a brain bleed, which is when protein builds up in the blood vessels until they burst.

I immediately got on the next plane back to Boston to be with my mother. It was a nerve-wracking flight, but when I arrived, I learned that the situation wasn't dire. The doctors were confident that she would recover and she was soon released from the hospital. My concerns were alleviated but we weren't out of the woods yet.

Unless you've lived with a friend or loved one who has short-term memory loss, it's a difficult thing to explain. When you first witness the symptoms, it's unnerving. This happened to me when I took my mother to a brunch buffet one afternoon. She took a walk around to look at the spread and returned with a sticky bun. She loved those things. Before we left, I suggested she go back up one last time to see if she wanted anything else. She walked back up to the buffet and came back with another sticky bun.

"Mom, you just had one of those," I said.

"Oh? I did?" she asked.

At that moment, I started to understand what was wrong. Things got worse around Christmas. The whole family was sitting around the dinner table when I put a plate of ravioli in front of my mother. A couple of minutes later, she asked me for the plate.

"Mom, it's right in front of you," I said.

This time it wasn't a matter of her forgetting. The plate was just off to the right side of the table and she couldn't see it because she had lost sight in her right eye. She was doing her best to manage her situation, but she didn't really know what was going on either. It slowly became clear that she could not live at her house alone.

I started traveling back and forth between Miami and Fall River more frequently. I'd spend a week in Miami and then a week at home as my brother and I looked for a facility where our mother could live. It couldn't be just anywhere. Luckily, my brother and his wife were able to take care of her and check in on her when I wasn't there. I give them both a lot of credit for doing most of the heavy lifting while Mom's living situation was in limbo.

We found a wonderful facility in Somerset. Anyone who has gone through this process knows how heartbreaking it can be. No matter how beautiful the place, it's always difficult, and it was one of the hardest things I've ever had to do in my life. I visited every chance I got but I always had to fly back to Miami and I felt like a failure as a son.

In July 2014, I received another dreadful call from my brother. He told me that the staff at the retirement home had found my mother after she had fallen in her room. It turned out that she had suffered another brain bleed. She was at Brigham and Woman's Hospital in Boston and on life support.

I hopped on the next flight to Boston and went right to the hospital. My mother was unconscious but I was able to spend time with her and hold her hand. She may not have been responsive but it felt like she knew we were there. When her friend, Grace, made a joke, I swear that I saw a small smile cross her face. In spite of the horrific circumstances, that was comforting.

A friend who lived across the street from Fenway Park was out of town on a road trip and left me his keys so I could stay at his place instead of trekking back and forth from my brother's house in Fall River. I spent the majority of my time at the hospital, but I needed some time to clear my head. I used to wake up early and run through the streets of Boston. Sometimes, I'd get a day pass to a local gym and get in a quick workout before heading over to the hospital.

I spent a week at her bedside. I'd talk to her and try to make her as comfortable as possible, but I knew she was dying and that was absolute torture. I felt helpless, but the staff at the hospital was incredible. I couldn't have asked for more.

One afternoon, the doctor explained to my brother and me that the chances of my mother ever making a full recovery were next to impossible. We had prepared ourselves for the possibility but to hear him actually say it made it real. There was no coming back for her. We made the difficult decision to take her off life support. It felt like my heart was being ripped out of my chest.

True to form, my mom fought to stay alive for two days. Nobody who knew her was surprised. She had a TV in her room, and her head was tilted to the right so I sat on that side in case she opened her eyes. One night, when my brother was at work and I was alone with her, I noticed her breathing start to slow down. Her breaths almost felt like contractions. First, they were 20 seconds apart, then 30 seconds. There were a few moments when I thought she had passed away and then she would breathe again. Finally, she turned her head away from me, shed a single tear, and stopped breathing. It honestly felt like she knew I was there. When I told the nurse what happened, she said it was a documented phenomenon known as The Angel's Kiss.

My mother was loved by the people of Fall River but I never truly understood her impact on others until the funeral. So many people came, all of them telling me what an incredible person she was. I must have received hundreds of texts and messages on Facebook. I heard so many great stories, particularly about how my mother would always go out of her way to take care of other people. She could sense when someone was uncomfortable in a group and in those situations, she would always take attention off that person and put it on herself. It was something I watched my mother do for years and it was comforting to hear that others picked up on it as well.

That whole year, my mother had been telling me that she just wanted to hang on long enough to be there for the wedding. "Don't worry, you'll be there," I told her many times, but she never got to see my wedding. That was absolutely heartbreaking.

My mother passed away in July 2014 and Melanie and I married in September at Tropicana Field, right there on the grass where the Tampa Bay Rays play. We got the idea from Randy Frankel when Melanie and I joined him in his box earlier in the year.

"You guys should get married here," he said.

I liked the idea from the beginning but when I turned to Melanie, I could tell by the look on her face that she was not as keen. As time went on, the idea grew on her. A baseball stadium definitely made a unique location for a wedding ceremony. As soon as she was on board, Randy set it up. My brother Mike was my best man. We had a modest ceremony with about 150 people and it was beyond our wildest dreams.

There were tremendous highs and lows squeezed into those few months. It was bittersweet and a little surreal to marry the woman I loved so shortly after the passing of my mother. My mom would have loved the ceremony and I know she adored Melanie.

Years earlier, Jim Reid had told me, "Marry someone just like your mother."

I'm happy to say that I did. I feel so lucky to have found someone who is kind, caring, and truly happy. I couldn't ask for more. When I'm with her I feel like I've won the lottery. The sun rises and sets with her.

WHAT I LEARNED

Never take your friends and family members for granted. Losing a loved one is a horrible experience, but life is a rollercoaster ride. Nothing will ever fill the void left by the death of someone close, but there is something wonderful and positive waiting around the corner if you can stay strong and make it through the bad times.

CHAPTER 15

ANATOMY AND BEYOND

"Culture is not just one thing. It's everything. Culture is not static, it's dynamic. Everyone on your team creates it and you are creating it each day by what you think, say, and do. You can elevate it by what you think, improve it by what you say, and make it great by what you do."

—Jon Gordon, author

On December 4, 2014, a few months after I got married, Anatomy opened its doors.

The one thing any new gym owner worries about is being able to attract members. They're the lifeblood of any facility and we wanted to get people in the door and show them what we had to offer. Once people saw all the added services, we knew they would believe in our gym and want to join. How many gyms provide massage therapy, IVs, and have a chiropractor on staff?

I had a roster of 30 clients who trained anywhere from one to four times a week. My partners asked me if those clients would come to Anatomy. I honestly didn't think any of them would. I really didn't. People aren't typically married to their trainer; they're married to their routine. But several familiar faces ended up proving me wrong. When Audrey Bennati made the move and joined Anatomy, it started to feel like we were officially a gym.

I was flattered by the support and thankful for the members who immediately signed up, but it wasn't all because of me. It was because of the atmosphere and energy our team created in the gym. That's the result of a strong staff. Building a business was a different type of challenge for me, but luckily, we surrounded ourselves with a lot of smart people who had experience and knew the industry inside and out. My role as the head of fitness and wellness was to hire all the trainers. They had to be humble, hardworking, and caring.

A gym is supposed to be an enjoyable environment but it turns out that most gyms are confrontational. I thought back to the days when I first started training and how good it felt when one of the older guys told me to keep it up and gave me encouragement. I wanted to create an environment that allowed everyone to feel comfortable, confident, and secure. Equinox was a global brand but the people weren't friendly. That's not a knock on Equinox but it's how most gyms are these days. When a place gets bigger, it's hard to hold onto what made that place special in the beginning.

We wanted people who were happy, passionate, and liked to work. We wanted trainers who were going to help the members, regardless if they were their clients or not. In other gyms, trainers won't give you the time of day if you don't train with them. Some won't even say hello. I wanted Anatomy to be the kind of place where someone drags themselves out of bed and goes even when they're feeling down because they're addicted to the energy. Not every client who walks into the gym is looking for a high five. Some don't smile or even look up, but we're there and the training is available if they need it.

The trainers were the ones on the floor working closely with the clients but we wanted everyone on the staff to have the same positive energy. That goes for me just as much as it goes for the person working the front desk. The front desk person was important because that person sets the tone for the entire club. The single best way to ensure that the floor of a gym isn't dead is to have great staff. The right atmosphere was critical because people are turned off by clubs that lack energy and respect for others. That made the hiring process important and we made sure to hire quality people. We as a team had to collectively agree on every single hire. We were not necessarily looking for the best people, we were looking for the right people.

Back when I was at Equinox, I thought we had a great training staff and asked one of the managers if he thought our success was attributable to the team.

He looked me in the eye and said, "It's not about the team. It's about the system."

They weren't trying to keep the trainers down at Equinox but they weren't promoting them either.

I came from the athletic world and played for coaches like Bill Parcells, Bill Belichick, Pete Carroll, and Dick LeBeau. If you ask a coach that same question, they will say that it's about the team and not the plays. It was that attitude that inspired my business model. Equinox may be about the system but Anatomy is about the team. Our system is great but we can't do what we do without the team.

I push our team to be their best but in a different way. The experience I had as a high school, college, and professional football player took a psychological toll on me. I don't think it was productive and that's why we have a no yelling policy at Anatomy. Could I handle yelling? Yeah. Do I think it's the best way to do business? Probably not. I've seen business owners scream at employees in front of staff and it ends up costing them employees. Nobody wants to go to work if they hate the environment.

I try to lead by example and maintain open lines of communication. If there is a problem with one of my staff members, I want to talk to that person immediately so the problem doesn't fester. I also ask for their feedback. I don't know it all. I don't have all the answers and sometimes I have to check myself, but I do have the best interests of my staff in mind. I would hope that if anyone needed anything, I would help them. Even if it's not in the best interest of my business, I'd want to help them because so many people helped me along the way. I don't want to stand in their way. I want to be the person who bridges gaps.

It may sound crazy but we know when we've done a good job with our trainers when they move on to different opportunities. That's the best-case scenario. When you promote your trainers and encourage them to grow, you have to let go. The alternative is that they stay and don't grow at all. That's not good for us and it's not good for them.

However, we want the clients to stay and most of them have stayed. I've

Culture is everything with the Anatomy traning team.

Mel is my superwoman,
and light of my life.

Almost 10 years after my first cover,
and looking more confident.

been training many of my clients for more than a decade—in fact, most are still in the same time slots. That comes from building a rapport. It comes from being consistent and being dependable. You do that by being on time, being responsible, and doing what you say you will. You have to be supportive and look them in the eye. Tell them when they did a good job, and at the same time, let them know when there is an area where they can improve. You have to be open to how each client responds. No two are the same and everybody has different strengths and weaknesses. You will make mistakes but view those mistakes as lessons. View success as the midpoint, not the conclusion, and see where you can go from there. You train, assess, reassess, apply what you know, use what works, and throw away what doesn't.

I own a gym and work as a personal trainer but there is so much more to what I do than the physical workout. The mental component is just as important. In fact, if you don't have the right outlook and mindset, you will never achieve your training goals. What does mobility matter if you're feeling depressed? Who cares how much you can squat or bench press if you feel terrible about your life? Once you get your head straight and feel good mentally, you can start to improve your body. I know that from firsthand experience; I've been down and out, and I witnessed the power of positive thinking.

When I tore my knee in Montreal, I was depressed. I was stuck in my condo with nothing more than a couch and a large TV. I would get up to do my rehab and I worked hard, but the rest of the time I just sat there. I felt like a prisoner. During those weeks, I spent hours on the computer and I found myself gravitating toward inspirational and motivational books and videos on YouTube. I made a connection with the guys in those videos. I was tired of being in pain. I didn't know if I would play again and I was ready to give up, but when I connected with people who inspired and motivated me, I felt good. I felt hopeful. I started to play the videos in the background while I did my rehab. When I recovered and could leave the condo, I got an MP3 player and had them converted to audio files so I could listen with my headphones during the day. Understanding how others worked through adversity to become their best inspired me. I became hooked.

Having a positive mindset is also important because it's infectious. It

One of our first dates.
She's my everything.

Our wedding day. Mel carries us both in any photo.

Doing our best to make our impact in fitness.

Randy always looks out for me.

impacts you and it affects others. When I learned that I couldn't play football anymore, I started posting positive quotes online every day. That was my therapy and my medicine, and I began to get messages from people who said my positivity inspired them. Little did they know that I was doing it to hold myself together. Their responses surprised me but also gave me a jolt that rippled through everything I did. Slowly, my perspective started to change. You say it, you believe it, you live it, and then it becomes your whole outlook on life.

When I first arrived in Miami, I started listening to a speech on YouTube by motivational speaker and author, Eric Thomas. He said, "When you want to succeed as bad as you want to breathe, then you'll be successful." A native of Detroit, Michigan, he wasn't polished but he was passionate. He spoke about being homeless and how it took him 12 years to get a four-year degree. I laughed when I heard that because he sounded just like me.

He said, "I'm the turtle and not the rabbit."

He may have gotten off to a slow start but he eventually graduated college and then went on to earn a master's degree and a PhD. The guy went through adversity but quickly evolved into an influencer who now speaks to packed houses and NFL teams.

I could relate to what he was saying because it felt like he understood me. He sounded like Marc Megna. That first year in Miami, I must have listened to his speeches thousands of times. It reminded me of all the kids who were supposedly the smartest in high school or the best athletes in college and how I eventually surpassed most of them. It's hard to beat a person who doesn't give up. But if you were to tell my 12-year-old self that I would eventually defy the odds and play in the NFL, becoming the man I am today, I wouldn't have believed it.

Most kids look up to the NFL players they watch on TV and never see that kind of potential in themselves. I know I never did, and that's why I gravitated to public speaking over the years. Sure, right now I'd love to be able to expand my business and open up Anatomy facilities all over the country but what most people don't realize is that a gym or fitness center is not the most profitable business. It's more of a long-term investment or, in my case, a life purpose. I believe I've been placed on this earth to inspire people and show them what is possible with hard work and dedication.

NFL organizations always arrange speaking gigs for the players. When I first started to play with the Patriots, there was an event at a high school that Willie McGinest couldn't fit into his schedule. They asked if I wanted to go in his place. I jumped at the chance and told them to put me down for anything.

"You don't even need to ask me," I said. "I'll go anywhere and speak."

A lot of times, I could tell that 90 percent of the high schoolers weren't paying attention. They were kids so that was expected, but I also knew that I could have an impact on the other 10 percent who were paying attention. I knew that because I was one of those kids. My mom worked several jobs and my dad wasn't around, so I was excited to listen to any adult who made time to speak to me. I hung on every word. That's what drew me to it and that's why I kept doing it.

Years later, when I was playing football in Montreal, a teacher approached me to see if I would be interested in public speaking. She was a huge Alouettes fan and I was a new player who got a lot of attention because of my time in the NFL. She thought the local kids would benefit from hearing me speak. I ended up crafting two different speeches—one about hard work and another about being bullied as a child.

I didn't really know what I was doing. It usually took me about 30 minutes to warm up and hit my stride but I got better. Speaking to kids in Montreal allowed me to get my feet wet. I did up to 40 speeches during the off season. I even went home to Fall River to speak at Durfee and talk to the football team. Word of mouth spread and I went on to speak at universities in Florida and kids at a youth correctional facility in Miami. I had different troubles than those kids but I could identify with them because a lot of people had ruled me out just like them.

Speakers like Tony Robbins and Eric Thomas inspire the world on a daily basis. I hope that I can have a fraction of the positive impact that they've had on people. Still, I learned early on not to emulate them. I'm mindful of my story and who I am. My experience is unique and my personal perspective makes the message more impactful.

The first thing I try to do when speaking to any audience is to help them realize that I didn't always look the way I do now. I wasn't always 6'2" and 220 pounds. I wasn't always strong or fast, and I definitely wasn't as emotionally stable. I didn't have the motivation and I didn't have focus. I also wasn't handed anything. People see that I own a gym and say, "Well, of course you own a gym because you know powerful people."

"Okay, well how did I meet those people?" I ask.

"You played in the NFL so you have connections."

"Okay, well how did I get to the NFL?"

"You got a scholarship to college and made it to the pros," they say.

I continue, "Okay, how did I get that scholarship?"

There is always a certain amount of luck involved but that works both ways. People who are successful create opportunities and put themselves in the position to succeed because they work their ass off.

I had to work for everything and it's the same for most people. It all starts with figuring out what it is you want to do. Learn as much as possible about it. Research successful people and see how they got to where they are. Then, come up with a plan. That plan becomes the process. Learn how to love the process because there are no shortcuts. Break that bigger goal down into smaller mini-goals. Every mini-goal you achieve builds a new layer of confidence. Have it in your mind that you can't be stopped.

The tricky part is that you never really know when you've achieved success. It's not a single destination. There is always something more to improve or achieve. All you can do is what you feel is best and what you feel is right. Keep your head down, go to work, and see what happens. If it feels good, keep going. If it doesn't, you might have to change course. When that happens, you'll know when the time is right to make an adjustment. Value the opinions of those closest to you but focus on how you feel and listen to yourself.

The ancillary benefit of diving into the process is that you gain invaluable knowledge and experience. You learn what it takes to achieve something and that is something very few people understand. It's not just about hard work but it's about making good decisions and developing good habits. That's what puts you in a better place to succeed and allows you to improve.

One story I often tell is about the pictures of athletes I used to put all over my bedroom walls. What I never realized at the time was that I was creating what was known as a vision board. That was the first thing I'd see at night and the last thing I'd see before I went to bed. During the day, I pictured myself on the field. I saw myself making extraordinary plays and being the hero. I actually sat on the floor of my room and walked through each step of a game. I could smell the freshly cut grass. I could feel the texture of the ball. I saw myself sacking the quarterback and then making a game-saving interception as time ran out on the clock. I did that for thousands of hours.

Those habits soon became second nature. When I got to the University of Richmond, that was what gave me a competitive edge. Every single moment when I was not on the field or in the classroom was spent visualizing game-time scenarios. I saw myself rushing the passer, knocking down the lineman's hands, and punching the ball out of the running back's arm while I dragged him down from behind. I saw myself flying off the ball when it was snapped. I did that over and over again. Those mental reps, combined with the repetition instilled by Coach Cullen during practice, allowed me to know everything that was going to happen before it unfolded on the field. I had already played out every possible scenario in my head hundreds of times so there were no surprises during the game. When the ball was snapped, I was there instantly. It almost wasn't fair. If you can't picture yourself achieving a goal, then you will probably never achieve it. Imagining yourself a certain way is the first step to becoming that person.

I don't have the mystique of a star like Bledsoe or McGinest. Kids would always rather have those guys come to their school and speak but I bring something different to the table. I learned that kids could identify with Marc Megna more than they could with a superstar like Bledsoe, who is far removed from their lives.

I may not have been raised in poverty, but I wasn't special and I wasn't born into anything. My family went through our share of tough times. I was a blue-collar kid from Fall River who built himself up with hard work. I was told that I wasn't big enough, fast enough, strong enough, or smart enough. Even though I wasn't as skilled as the guy next to me, I made sure that I was better prepared so I could outperform him. That was the secret to my success. If I could do it so can other kids who come from humble beginnings and are being counted out. When I go to a school to speak, I want them to look at me and say, "I can be like that, too!"

Everything changes the moment you start thinking like that. Having self-confidence and believing in yourself is a necessary part of the process. Nobody in the world can stop you from achieving your dreams except for yourself. The ball is in your court. There are actions that you can take today to change the course of your life. Every day matters.

I speak at events for the same reason that I started training—to help people. That's the same reason why I write, and it's the reason why I started The Megna Method podcast. So much of the content I produce today is motivational and not science-based or exercise-specific. Of course, I do create content around fitness and training programs but I think of that as secondary.

I love everything about what I do, especially working with people. I never set out to open up some monster chain of fitness centers or get myself on the cover of a bunch of magazines. Everyone has a different version of success but success is as simple as hearing from someone that I've had a positive impact on their life. When someone tells me that they were inspired by something I shared or did, that inspires me to be better.

Life to me is about helping people. There are no self-made men. I wouldn't be where I am today if I didn't have others helping me along the way. Now it's my turn to pay that forward and help people through the rough patches in their lives by using my life as an example. I want to pass on information and inspire people to do things they never thought were possible. If they can use that knowledge to succeed themselves and to help others, slowly the world will become a better place.

WHAT I LEARNED

Being a winner isn't about you winning. Being a true winner is about inspiring others and becoming our best selves. My athletic career ended over a decade ago, and I found a tremendous amount of enjoyment and satisfaction when competing but it doesn't compare to the satisfaction I now experience when taking the lead to inspire and give back to others.

CPSIA information can be obtained
at www.ICGtesting.com
Printed in the USA
FSHW021726181019
63101FS

9 781733 474900